Eight Domains of Phenomenology and Research Methods

Eight Domains of Phenomenology and Research Methods is a unique text that explains how the foundational literature representing our life-world experience aligns theory with research methods.

Maintaining focus on the core problem of phenomenological investigations, the author strives to bridge theory with applied research by critically reviewing examples from the applied literature. With the extensive use of the foundational literature's original voices, the book elaborates on how renowned scholars such as Husserl, Heidegger, and Sartre argued their ideas. A range of diverse voices is also explored through the perspectives of feminist and Black phenomenologists. The text then goes on to unpack the phenomenological methodologies with detailed explanations of signature techniques, hereunder the epoché and reduction from the perspectives of transcendental phenomenology, phenomenological psychology, and genetic (generative) phenomenology. Finally, it addresses the problem of articulating phenomenological research questions as well as interview questions that align with the different domains and methodologies.

This book is a must read for postgraduate students, dissertation students, and qualitative researchers interested in conducting phenomenological research within social psychology, sociology, and education.

Henrik Gert Larsen is a phenomenology expert. He is an alumnus of the University of Copenhagen and the Chicago School of Professional Psychology. His experience includes chairing dissertations and teaching qualitative research. He has also authored books on phenomenological research and development and application.

Eight Domains of Phenomenology and Research Methods

Henrik Gert Larsen

Routledge
Taylor & Francis Group

LONDON AND NEW YORK

First published 2023
by Routledge
4 Park Square, Milton Park, Abingdon, Oxon OX14 4RN

and by Routledge
605 Third Avenue, New York, NY 10158

Routledge is an imprint of the Taylor & Francis Group, an informa business

© 2023 Henrik Gert Larsen

The right of Henrik Gert Larsen to be identified as author of this work has been asserted in accordance with sections 77 and 78 of the Copyright, Designs and Patents Act 1988.

British Library Cataloguing-in-Publication Data
A catalogue record for this book is available from the British Library

ISBN: 978-1-032-21797-0 (hbk)
ISBN: 978-1-032-21800-7 (pbk)
ISBN: 978-1-003-27005-8 (ebk)

DOI: 10.4324/9781003270058

Typeset in Times New Roman
by SPi Technologies India Pvt Ltd (Straive)

Contents

1 Introduction

The problems the phenomenological literature is concerned with are not well articulated in the secondary literature. Often, phenomenology is boiled down to a single inductive method, and readers will encounter catchphrases such as "the meaning of the lived experience" or "the essence of the lived experience," but stating that you are researching "lived experiences" and interviewing subjects does not on its own produce phenomenological findings.

In his famous preface to *Phenomenology of Perception*, Merleau-Ponty (1978, p. vii) provided a definition of phenomenology (i.e., the study of essence). Merleau-Ponty pointed to several research themes, for example, the essence of consciousness, the essence of perception, or the essence stemming from human existence in the world. However, his explanation underscores the heterogeneous nature of the field rather than providing a clarification of the subject matter itself, and in contrast, Heidegger (2010) argued that phenomenology should be conceived more in terms of a method, which does not designate "the objects of its research" (pp. 32–33).

Although the seminal authors have different definitions of phenomenology, a common theme is that the meaning of reality must be understood from the first-person point of view. Thus, it is our reality because we live it, and Merleau-Ponty stated that "no world whatsoever is conceivable that is not thought by someone" (Edie, 2000, p. 57). Consequently, Merleau-Ponty (1978) argued that "all my knowledge of the world, even my scientific knowledge, is gained from my own particular point of view, or from some experience of the world without which the symbols of science would be meaningless" (p. viii).

In this connection, Husserl (2017, p. 425) concluded that phenomenology is focused on the problem of constitution (Konstitutionsprobleme) and argued that "the comprehensive task of constitutive phenomenology"

DOI: 10.4324/9781003270058-1

is "the elucidation of the whole interpretation of the operation of consciousness which leads to the constitution of a possible world" (Husserl, 1973b, p. 50). In this manner, the axiom of phenomenological research can be boiled down to "the world, then, and the being of that which is to be found in the world, are concretely understood when they are understood as constituted" (Fink, 1995, p. li).

However, phenomenology is distinct from psychology. Where the psychologist primarily focuses on how an exterior reality affects the mind, then the phenomenologist presupposes that this reality is not actual but a "constituted objectification" (Marion, 1998, p. 2) and is therefore interested in the "problems of phenomenological shaping" (Husserl, 2017, p. 425) of reality. Husserl (2017, p. 23) credited Brentano with discovering that consciousness is intentional and being conscious is therefore always being conscious of something (Husserl, 1977, p. 22), and intentionality has its own immanent objectification that shapes our experience of the world in certain ways (Zahavi, 2007, p. 70).

Merleau-Ponty claimed that intentionality is the main discovery of phenomenology (Merleau-Ponty, 1978, p. xvii), but here we are immediately confronted with the fact that Husserl's fellow phenomenologists defined intentionally in very different ways and consequently took their considerations of the constitution problem in very different directions.

The gist of the disagreement within the phenomenological tradition can be boiled down to whether essentia or existentia has priority. In other words, should the phenomenological investigation focus on subjectivity or comportment (behaviors)? This schism is clearly illustrated by the disagreements between Husserl and his most prominent student Heidegger. For example, Husserl (Sheehan, 2007) expressed grave reservations about Heidegger's articulation of phenomenology in *Being and Time*, published in 1927, and in private correspondence stated,

> I really have to regret that, as regards method and content, his work (and his lecture courses too, for that matter) seem to be essentially different from my works and courses; in any event, up to this point there still exists no bridge between him and me that the students we share in common can cross.

(p. 385)

Finally, around 1929, Husserl concluded that he could no longer include Heidegger's work within the framework of his phenomenology (Fink, 1995, p. xi).

Consequently, the notion of a unified phenomenological research paradigm is one of the first myths we must dispel. According to Heidegger (1988), "[T]here is no such thing as one phenomenology" (p. 328), and in this spirit, I will consider eight specific domains of phenomenological theory and aligned methods. Specifically, I will consider how the foundational literature articulates and examines the problem of what it means for something to be real.

2 Review of the Seminal Methodological Literature

Moustakas and Empathy

Within the applied literature, one of the best-known works may be Moustakas's (1994) *Phenomenological Research Methods*. This book is wrapped in Husserlian phenomenology and offers the reader an authentic definition of intentionality as being synonymous with consciousness (p. 59). Nevertheless, Moustakas took considerable poetic license with the foundational literature. For example, Moustakas (1994, p. 85) explained that the epoché is a process of setting aside personal biases and engaging in reflections about what the research subjects are disclosing. This is obviously not the case, and as any casual reading of Husserl's works would reveal, the purpose of the epoché is to put the natural attitude out of play.

Moustakas (1994, p. 41) revealed that his version of the phenomenological method is equally inspired by his background as a therapist and stated that "the method through which the other becomes accessible to me is that of empathy" (p.37). It is not uncommon to see researchers with a background in therapy apply themselves in a manner where they essentially co-construct meanings with their subjects, and Giorgi (2006) pointed out that Moustakas's research typically emulates a therapy format because most of Moustakas's cases only include a single subject. Nevertheless, the question is whether empathy can be defended as a method of what Zahavi (2007) calls the "conceptual problem of other minds" (p. 68).

Relatedly, Max Scheler, in his seminal work *The Nature of Sympathy* (1954), stated, "[I]t is a fundamental weakness of theories, which seek to derive our knowledge of other minds from inferences or processes of empathy" (p. 251). Scheler explained that "the theory of empathy offers no grounds for assuming the existence of other selves, let alone other individuals. For it can only serve to confirm the belief that it is

DOI: 10.4324/9781003270058-2

my self, which is present all over again, and never that this self is other and different from my own" (p. 242).

Thus, Moustakas's reliance on empathy as a method for overcoming the barriers between his mind and the minds of others may suffer from what William James identified as the "psychologist's fallacy," where the researcher confounds their frame of reference with their subjects (Ashworth, 2009).

Moustakas's (1994) work is an idiosyncratic presentation of the phenomenological research approach and is positioned outside of the established traditions. Although Moustakas references Husserl's main works, he fails to make any connections with the deep body of methodological and applied literature that came out of the Dutch and Duquesne schools, and researchers using his approach will therefore find themselves producing research outside of the applied phenomenological psychological tradition.

Giorgi and Psychological Subjectivity

Giorgi (1985, 2009) offered a different take on Husserlian-inspired phenomenological research. In *Phenomenology and Psychological Research* and *The Descriptive Phenomenological Method in Psychology: A Modified Husserlian Approach*, Giorgi's take on the psychological phenomenological method is sometimes referred to as the Duquesne School, from the university where it first took root in the United States, or simply existential phenomenology. The Duquesne School was motivated by the need to establish rigorous procedures for qualitative psychological research grounded in the phenomenological literature (Englander & Morley, 2021). In this respect, it is aligned with the Dutch School, which aimed at a phenomenological clarification of the basic psychological concepts (Kockelmans, 1987).

However, Giorgi (2009) decided to emphasize the term *descriptive* for the purpose of reminding researchers not to colonize their research with extant theoretical perspectives and instead focus on the data (Englander & Morley, 2022). In this manner, Giorgi stays true to Husserl's (2017) axiom that "self-evident data are patient, they let theories chatter about them, but remain what they are. It is the business of theories to conform to the data" (p. 89).

Giorgi (2009, p. 184) posited that psychological subjectivity is a form of intentionality and therefore relevant for the study of essence, and ultimately, Giorgi's (2009) project is to illuminate the subjects' "psychological reality" (p. 184). Thus, Giorgi's approach is a modification of Husserl's transcendental method. In this connection, Keirby (1997) argued that Husserl's methods aim at an "illumination accessible only to the individual who performs the reduction" (p. 208). This position seems to be congruent with Husserl's views in *Ideas: General Introduction to Pure Phenomenology*, where he stated, "[W]e have primordial experience of ourselves and our states of consciousness in the so-called inner or self-perception not of others" (Husserl, 2017, p. 51). However, when Husserl made these statements, he was attempting to develop a scientific philosophy, and therefore they should not be construed as an argument against the possibilities of descriptive psychology.

Thus, Merleau-Ponty (Edie, 2000) argued that nothing in Husserl's phenomenological theory prohibits the elucidation of the experience of another person as long as "I perceive him and his mode of behaviour" (p. 65) because in this situation, "the experience of researcher and subject are interrelated" (p. 65). In other words, the researcher is the principal instrument of illumination, and all thematic findings are ultimately derived from the phenomenological reflections of the researcher and not the subjects. In addition, Merleau-Ponty (Edie, 2000, p. 66) argued that "knowledge of facts is impossible without some insights into essence," and it can therefore be argued that the facticity of descriptive psychology also provides some insight into essence. Hence, Giorgi (2009) posited that by assuming the right psychological attitude, we can be aware of other people's emotional states without knowing their causes. To this end, Giorgi (2009) invoked a version of Husserl's eidetic method and stated that "the attitude of the scientific reduction and the attitude of heighten psychological sensitivity" (p. 190) allows the researcher to "understand humans in the world in a psychological way" (p. 190).

Giorgi (2009) is more attuned to the task of empirical research than Moustakas (1994). Giorgi (2009) essentially extrapolates on the eidetic method associated with Husserl's (1977) lectures on phenomenological psychology, where Moustakas ends up confounding phenomenological psychology with transcendental phenomenology. However, Giorgi (2009) relies on the same rationale as Moustakas by invoking techniques applied for "therapeutic situations" (p. 98). Nevertheless, Giorgi's approach departs from therapy as he advocates that phenomenological psychological research should include a larger sample than just one subject. In other words, the eidetic variations are moved out of the researcher's mind and into the empirical realm, where a variety of subjects and their perspectives ensure a background from which the phenomenon can stand out (Giorgi, 2006, 2009).

In the second half of his book, Giorgi (2009) demonstrated his methods with a study of jealousy. Paley (2017, p. 45) tore into Giorgi's work and questioned how he managed to identify and delimit the jealousy phenomenon and how he can know that the interview data describes said phenomenon. Paley's (2017) concerns were based on a misconception of phenomena and a misunderstanding of the research agenda of phenomenological psychology. When Giorgi (2009) referred to jealousy as a phenomenon, he was mistaken because jealousy is a psychological concept and not a phenomenon. A phenomenon is an appearance or a psychological act that lets something appear. However, the research agenda of phenomenological psychology is essentially an ontological clarification of basic psychological concepts (Kockelmans, 1987). However, Paley (2017) was not entirely off point with his critique, and Schutz (1972) pointed out that when researchers put a concept in the place of a phenomenon, they introduce an element of theoretical bias.

Subjectivism in Interpretative Phenomological Analysis (IPA) Research

In *Interpretative Phenomenological Analysis: Theory, Method and Research*, Smith et al. (2009) claimed to position subjectivity at the center of their phenomenological methodology. However, Smith et al. (2009) confounded subjectivity with subjectivism, when they suggested that IPA aims to illuminate the lived experiences of individual subjects "in their particular contexts, exploring their personal perspectives" (p. 32). In other words, they embraced standpoint epistemology when they argued that the meaning of an experience simply is what the subjects claim it is (p. 34). Hence, IPA does not transcend the subjects' existential situations, and consequently, Smith et al. (2009) find no utility in the epoché and reduction (Giorgi, 2011), which they (Smith et al., 2009) made clear with the following statement:

> For Husserl it was important to move from the individual instances to establish the eidetic structure or essence of experience. This is of course a noble aim. For IPA however, the prior task of detailed analysis of particular cases of actual life and lived experience remains the priority at this time.
>
> (p. 38)

By eschewing the epoché and reduction, we are left with mainly idiographic research outcomes, and Scheler (1973, p. xix) pointedly stated that "there may arise here and there a view according to which phenomenology deals only with isolated phenomena. ... I am completely removed from such picture-book phenomenology." Whether IPA, is picture-book phenomenology is not for this author to determine, but without the phenomenological signature methods, IPA researchers must assume that their subjects enjoy privileged access to the essence of their experiences. In this manner, IPA contradicts the tenets of Husserl's phenomenology by essentially elevating the natural standpoint to the arbiter of truth. The point being that the natural attitude deceives us by perpetuating the illusion that it is the external world that shapes our phenomenal experiences and not the other way around.

To overcome the trap of subjectivism, Smith et al. (2009) suggested that the data should be interpreted, and, to this end, they invoked Heidegger's phenomenology. However, it is not entirely clear how their notion of interpretation is particularly Heideggerian because Heidegger's existential phenomenology is not aimed at understanding the specificness of human experiences in particular contexts. Thus, Heidegger (Heidegger & Boss, 2001, p. 4) stated that

> the basic constitution of human existence may be called *Da-sein*, or being-in-the-world. Of course, in this context the *Da* of this *Da-sein* certainly does not mean what it does in the ordinary sense – a location near an observer.

Consequently, phenomenological scholars find it difficult to see how exactly Smith et al. (2009) used the phenomenological axioms (Zahavi, 2019), and in heated rebuttals, Giorgi (2011) went as far as protesting that IPA is just a generic qualitative method and that the homage to Husserl and Heidegger is merely an attempt at gaining methodological legitimacy.

Praxis and Intentionality

In contrast, Van Manen's (2016) *Phenomenology of Practice* reflects the schism between Husserl and Heidegger by alluding to a phenomenological knowledge that is pathic rather than gnostic. In other words, a transcendental knowledge that is acquired through practical engagement with the world (2007). Thus, *Phenomenology of Practice* aligns with "Heidegger's emphasis on Dasein's practical behaviour, the relation to itself, the others and the world" (Luft, 2005, p. 145). Along these lines, Van Manen (2016) introduced a range of phenomenological domains that are based on professional practices such as "phenomenological pedagogy" (p. 198) and phenomenological paediatrics" (p. 206).

Emblematic of Van Manen's (2016) writing style is a play with words, which from time to time obscures his message. For example, the first lines in Chapter 1: "This text is an invitation to openness, and an invitation of openness to phenomenologies of lived meaning, the meaning of meaning, and the originary sources of meaning" (p. 15), may leave the casual reader somewhat confused about the purpose of his book. Adding to this confusion is the introduction of methodological concepts that are largely of his own invention (Zahavi, 2018b). For example, his explanation of the epoché and phenomenological reduction appears to directly contradict the foundational literature. Thus, Van Manen (2016) stated that "the basic idea of the epoché and reduction is to return to the world as we live it in the natural attitude" (p. 222). In fact, the role of the epoché is the exact opposite (i.e., to bracket the natural attitude). Van Manen (p. 223) introduced the "heuristic epoché-reduction: Wonder" and argued that "at the most basic level the phenomenological reduction consists of the attitude or mood of wonder." In support, Van Manen cited Merleau-Ponty, but a closer read of Merleau-Ponty appears not to support the provenance of such a concept, as Merleau-Ponty (1978, p. viii) clearly stated that phenomenology is not an attitude or mood but that "phenomenology is accessible only through a phenomenological method."

In the final analysis, *Phenomenology of Practice* reaches deep into the foundational literature. However, this book falls short of accomplishing the task indicated in its title. Instead of a kaleidoscopic tour de force of all the corners of phenomenology, a focused attempt at naturalizing Heidegger's existential phenomenology through the elevation of professional practical engagement as the primary constitutive phenomena would have added invaluable contribution to applied research.

Postintentional Phenomenology and Interconnectedness

Vagle's *Crafting phenomenological research* (2018) brings together the different phenomenological schools in an accessible and sufficiently detailed presentation. For example, the Overview of *Methodological language* (pp. 12–17) is a useful reference for the novice researcher. Vagle's account of phenomenology is however not without problems. For example, he postulated that "early phenomenology assumes that consciousness is not contained in individual subjects, but out in the intentional relations between subjects and the world" (p. 39). It is not clear what he meant by early phenomenology because the only scholarly support for this position comes from citing himself. Nevertheless, he argued that "People in their everyday contact with the world bring into being intentionality" (p. 29) and that intentionality should be understood as interconnectedness to other people (p. 39).

What motivates this interpretation of intentionality appears to be Vagle's (2018) desire to make phenomenology more applicable to social research by extracting it from Husserl's transcendental framework (p. 129). Vagle combined phenomenology with poststructuralism and thereby proposes an entirely novel approach, which he calls "post-intentional phenomenology" (p.123). However, it is not entirely clear why an alignment with poststructuralism is required because Heidegger (2010, p 123) already expunged intentionality from transcendental phenomenology with his conceptualization of Dasein as care, a theme that is also taken up by other thinkers within the phenomenological tradition such as Schutz, Scheler, and Ricoeur. It is therefore puzzling that Vagle (2018) decided to reach toward poststructuralism instead of building on what existential phenomenology has to offer in terms of elucidating Being with others. In this way, it is fair to argue that adding a second metatheoretical framework to a phenomenological research design is complicating matters, as we are already wrestling with the diversity within phenomenology itself.

Critical Phenomenology: Intentionality as Intersectionality

In a nod to Husserl's sense of crisis in the natural sciences, critical phenomenologists postulate that we are in a new crisis of race, gender, and other identities, and in their foreword to the anthology *50 Concepts for a Critical Phenomenology*, Weiss et al. (2020) argued that classical phenomenology may have overlooked the role internalization of existing "structural, political and institutional inequities" (p. xiv) play in constituting reality. Thus, critical phenomenology frames political, judicial, and financial institutions as quasitranscendental structures in the sense that they are existing actualities, which on the surface appear neutral to race and gender, but in fact perpetuate norms and biases belonging to a White patriarchal worldview. By wielding its physical and economic power, the White patriarchy has succeeded in constituting a reality based on its values and interests, which everyone else must cope with, and therefore they interfere with women's and minorities' ability to constitute their existence as equally normative.

This work does not present a coherent approach to critical phenomenological research, but as an anthology, it allows the contribution of diverse perspectives. For example, Guenther (2020, p. 12) argued that critical phenomenology must rely on a conceptualization of intentionality based on Merleau-Ponty, who is more open to the idea of a reciprocal constitution of the world and subject than Husserl's transcendental phenomenology.

In contrast, Davies (2020) argued that "transcendental subjectivity must be redescribed in terms of intersectionality" of "race, gender and class" (p. 3) to remain a relevant research approach in light of today's inequity problems. It is however not entirely clear what Davies means when he argues that intersectionality of difference constitutes what we are (p. 8) because in the context of Husserl's transcendental phenomenology, race, gender, and class are ideal objects and already constitutive accomplishments of subjectivity. Thus, subjectivity is a priori to intersectionality. Davies's conceptualization would have been better served by turning to Dasein analysis, which does exactly what he intends "to see our identities, personal and public as intersectional phenomena" (p. 8). Consequently, Guenther (2020) acknowledged that "being-in-the-world offers a more promising starting point for critical phenomenology."

However, the following chapters will demonstrate that the existential tradition beginning with Sartre's (1992) seminal work *Being and Nothingness* was the intellectual breakthrough that set in motion feminist and Black existentialism with theoretical and methodological implications for critical phenomenology.

3 What Is a Phenomenon?

Heidegger (2010, p. 33) rhetorically asked, "What is it that phenomenology is to be let seen? What is it that is to be called phenomenon?" It is an important question to clarify because phenomenological researchers, as other scholars, must be able to define their domain and identify the objects of their research. In other words, if we are to study phenomena, we need a theoretical clarification of what they are and how they can be seen for the simple reason that empirical research must be theory driven.

A typical mistake researchers make is that they confound phenomena with ideal types. For example, when Creswell (2007) explains that phenomenology is the study of "the meaning for several individuals of their lived experiences of a concept or a phenomenon" (p. 62), we are left with the impression phenomena are abstractions such as racism, disability, marginalization, etc. However, these are not phenomena, but ideal objects through which we can objectify different types of situations and objects. Thus, Kockelmans and Jager (1967) stated, "[O] bjects such as concepts, statements, conclusions, truths and proofs are irreal entities" (p. 128) that are products of interpretive acts (p. 170) for the purpose of objectifying a range of possible experiences with real objects and situations.

The problem arises when the researchers reverse the reduction and posit the ideal type as a "free entity" (Schutz, 1972, p. 190) because it is not clear how exactly a researcher can use "ideal-typical concepts to penetrate to the subjective meaning of individuals?" (p. xxii). For example, how can the concepts of race, class, gender, and intersectionality really assist us in understanding what a person has in mind when acting in certain ways?

Some researchers may initiate their investigations with an "ideal type" to ensure that their research is guided by theory and to claim

DOI: 10.4324/9781003270058-3

that they are objective observers (Schutz, 1972, p. xxii). However, this approach introduces an element of deduction, without the guardrails of quantitative reasoning, and researchers may inadvertently stumble into conjecture as their analysis inadvertently discovers the shadow of the ideal types attached to the interview data as "precisely the meaning the interpreter is looking for" (p. 190). Consequently, positioning ideal types as the object of a phenomenological study creates confusion as to whether they represent an already elucidated meaning-essence or the theoretical bias of the social researcher (Schutz, 1972, p. xxii).

To avoid digressing into social constructivism, we must keep in mind that "the essential characteristic of a phenomenon consists in the fact that it is consciousness-of-its-object" (Kockelmans & Jager, 1967, p. 303), and, therefore, "the term phenomenon does not apply first nor only to the object that appears, but indeed to the lived experience in which and according to which it appears" (Marion, 1998, p. 53).

In contrast to Creswell, Giorgi (2009, p. 93) defined phenomena as "any object whatsoever considered insofar as it is viewed from perspective of consciousness." While Giorgi is not wrong, his definition is incomplete because the phenomenon that phenomenologists investigate is "the perspective" or the appearing and not the appearance itself. It is of course correct that our experiences have a phenomenal character, but phenomenologists do not subscribe to the notion that phenomena are just the appearances of an exterior world.

Phenomena: Immanence and Transcendence

Heidegger (2010) explained that the first step of a phenomenological analysis is to describe what appears in the world and what is happening with these appearances. For example, "Houses, trees, people, mountains, stars" (p. 63). However, Heidegger conceded that such descriptions are "obviously a pre-phenomenological business, which cannot be phenomenological relevant at all" (p. 63). The reason is that "phenomena are never appearances, but every appearance is dependent upon phenomena" (p. 28). Thus Heidegger (Heidegger & Boss, 2001) posited that "there are two kinds of phenomena: Ontic and ontological. Ontic phenomena are "perceptible, existing phenomena," where ontological phenomena are "non-sensory and imperceptible" (p. 6).

In this manner, we can say that an experience has two moments: (a) a moment of immanence and (b) a moment of transcendence. Immanence is something that the subject can perceive or at least conceive of as truly belonging to an appearance. For example, the perception of a clock in front of us. Here the clock-object is immanent to our phenomenal experience.

In contrast, transcendence is something connected with the phenomenal appearance of the clock, but not as such part of its perceptible structures. In other words, the transcendent is what the subject posits about the phenomenal experience (Sartre, 1992, p. 11). Consequently, Heidegger (2010) defined this transcendence as a phenomenon

> that does *not* show itself initially and for the most part, something that is *concealed* [*verbogen*] in contrast to what initially and for the most part does show itself. But, at the same time, it is something that essentially belongs to what initially and for the most part shows itself, indeed in such a way that it constitutes its meaning and ground.
>
> (p. 33)

The question that divides phenomenology is whether the transcendence that bestows meaning on phenomenal appearances is of a noetic or pathic character. In other words, whether consciousness is constitutive or relational (Sartre, 1992, p. 21). From Husserl's perspective, intentional acts give phenomena the way that we experience them. Thus Marion (1998, p. 52) states phenomena "give themselves as they appear only on condition of appearing in the mode that consciousness silently imposes on them." In contrast, Heidegger (1988) finds this notion "an absurdity" (p. 64) because it would require that a subject's consciousness is constituted in such a way that it "is capable of climbing out of its subject and over to the object" (Boss, 1982, p. 32). Nevertheless, the following will present eight distinct perspectives on the constitutive phenomena, which may assist the researcher in framing a phenomenological study.

The Phenomena of Givenness and Essence

Husserl's project was not psychology, and in *The Idea of Phenomenology*, Husserl (1973a) warned his readers, "One must guard himself from the fundamental confusion between the pure phenomenon in the sense of phenomenology, and the psychological phenomenon" (p. 33). By this, Husserl (2019) means that the psychologist "views lived experiences as psychical states of empirical persons, i.e., psycho-physical subjects, and uncovers relationships ... between them, and follows their development, formation and transformation" (p. 28). In contrast, he believed that phenomenology should only be preoccupied with reality "in so far as it is intended, represented, intuited or conceptually thought" (p. 28).

Thus, Husserl (1973a, p. 34) argued that it was necessary to understand the difference between the "pure phenomenon of the mental act" and the "psychological phenomenon" (p. 34). In other words, Husserl gave the act of experiencing priority over what is experienced. In this connection, Husserl made the philosophical distinction between the thinking act and what is being thought by introducing the two philosophical terms: Noesis and noema. Noesis refers to the *content* immanent to intentionality, which can be understood as how the act of thought is directed toward something (Drummond, 2003, p. 71).

The term *content* is somewhat misleading because we are here considering content in a philosophical and not empirical sense. In other words, intentionality gives reality to psychological subjectivity in a manner that allows reality to constitute in a particular way (Marion, 1998, p. 9). The act can therefore be said to have a certain "monothetic" (Husserl, 2017, p. 424) content or a constitutive essence. Thus, Husserl (2019) stated that intentional acts contain "a priori truths which belongs to moments constitutive of objectivity" (p. 29). For example, intentional acts such as "perceiving, feeling, desiring, aspiring, loving, believing," (Welton, 2003, p. 13) judging, appreciating, etc., all have specific objectifying essences that, according to Husserl (2017), phenomenologically shape the givenness of reality and all areas of knowledge and their associated "basic regional concepts" (p. 426).

Husserl is careful to point out that essence is not to be confused with constructs, concepts, or abstractions, which Husserl (2017) refers to as "invented phenomena" produced by "psychological analyses that are no analyses at all" (p. 89) The essence is to be understood as the "aboutness" of experiencing in contrast to the "whatness" of the experienced. In other words, the "aboutness" immanent to the act is the constitutive condition of "the possibility of experience (Erfahrung)" (Husserl, 2001, p. 74). For example, Husserl (2017) explained that "an object such as a material thing, this paper, for instance, as given in perceptual experience, is in principle other than an experience, a being of a completely different kind" (p. 117). Therefore, perception is the intentional act and the essence or aboutness of this act gives objects to cognition in three dimensions. Thus, the essence of perception is perspective, and perspective is the constitutive condition of perceptual experience.

The Phenomena of Perception and the World

The service of natural science is to demystify the human body. This has led to a situation where the body is misconceived as merely a vehicle sustaining the brain and that consciousness resides in the brain. From this follows that science tends to conceive of perception as something triggered by external stimuli.

However, Merleau-Ponty rejected the dualism between mind and body. Instead, he posited that consciousness is embodied and that we therefore cannot distribute certain experiences to the mind and others to the body. In other words, Merleau-Ponty (1978) argued that mind and body are "an all-inclusive" (p. 124) and consequently that our lifeworld is experienced in action rather than thought (Edie, 2000, p. 12). From this insight follows that perception is an embodied intentionality (Edie, 2000, p. 3), and the world is "not what I think, but what I live through" (Merleau-Ponty, 1978, p. xvii). It is therefore not the ego that constitutes our lifeworld, but the unity of the living body and consciousness.

Consequently, perception is lived and not thought (Merleau-Ponty, 1978, p. xvii), and Merleau-Ponty argued that the embodied perception holds primacy over all other modalities of consciousness (Edie, 2000, p. 25) because it provides "the background from which all acts stand out" (Merleau-Ponty, 1978, pp. x–xi). Thus, Merleau-Ponty argued that "the perceived world is the always presupposed foundation of all rationality, all value and all existence" (Edie, 2000, p. 13). These insights lead him to formulate the axiom that the body "is our point of view of the world" (p. 5) and that "all its functions contribute to the perception of objects" (Edie, 2000, p. 5). Therefore, the body is a "knowing body" (Merleau-Ponty, 1978, p. 325), in the sense that it is the stabilizing structure of human existential comportment (p. 320) that in turn constitutes the world as a lived world.

The Phenomena of Apperception and the Lifeworld

Husserl (2017) argued that time consciousness is constitutive of the experience of our lifeworld as it binds "experience with experiences" (p. 236) and thereby creates "a continuous chain of retentions of retentions" (p. 237). In similar fashion, we find a movement in the opposite direction of protention where the "ego's temporal glance" (p. 237) apprehends what is being foreshadowed in what just transpired. In other words, our experience horizon contains both "retentional and anticipative features" (Fréchette, 2017, p. 78). Thus, Husserl (1977) explained that "the only genuine concept of the natural world-experience or of the experienced world, as we find it by looking back from now or any prior now or by looking ahead in any future now" (p. 46).

Hence, an experience is not a case of "a now," but a phenomenon constituted by "three dimensions of before, after and at the same time" (Husserl, 2017, p. 239). Thus, Husserl (2019) explained that the experience of a situation we find ourselves in or the "now-point" always includes a "consciousness of what has just been" (p. 54) and is likewise "animated by protentions" (p. 76) of what may come, and therefore "no concrete experience can pass as independent in the full sense of the term." Husserl (1970) defined this phenomenon as "apperception" (p. 320), and Barber (2015) explained that the term combines "ad (to) and perception, and hence apperception signifies all we bring to perception" (p. 28).

These additional data that apperception add to the perception come in the form of "analogizing apperceptions" where similar events from the past form a nexus with the immediate apprehended while in the same moment a nexus is established with "indicative apperceptions" containing a foreshadowing of what may come next (Geniusas, 2020, p. 196). Lambeth (2020) therefore posited that time consciousness is constitutive of how we transform the perceived world into a personal lifeworld (Lebenswelt) and therefore that the psychological phenomenon "apperception is fundamentally temporal" (p. 51)

However, in our natural attitude, we do not experience the temporality of our apperception because in the very moment our ego takes possession of a perception, our temporal horizon collapses into a single apperceptive perspective (Husserl, 1977, p. 44), where everything past, present, and future is experienced as a moment pertaining to the now-point (Husserl, 1977, p. 45), as if this bonus content that clings to the fringes of our immediate experience was already part of it to begin with (Geniusas, 2020, p. 187). In this manner, apperception fulfills a constitutive role by animating lived experiences (perceptions) with data not directly connected with what is apprehended. Thus, Geniusas (2020) concluded that it is "fully legitimate to define experiences as a synthetic unity of perceptions and apperceptions" (p. 192), and Chernavin (2016) elevated apperception to "the universal law for the formation of experience" (p. 53).

The Phenomenon of Care and Being

Dasein is often translated with "being there," which is literally correct, but still somewhat misleading. "Da" does mean "there," but Heidegger did not mean the specific coordinates of the living body. Instead, he thought of "being there" in terms of a care which is a relating to things and to others. Thus, Heidegger (2010, p. 117) explained that "Dasein in itself is essentially being with" and that "Being with existentially determines Dasein even when an other is not factically present and perceived" (p. 117). Consequently, Heidegger (1988) believed that Husserl's epistemological conceptualization of essence was a misunderstanding and argued that the essence of perception and all other intentional acts is not givenness, but "the relating itself" (p. 66). Sartre (1991) elaborated that "man and the world are relative beings, and the principle of their being is the relation" (p. 407). Therefore, Heidegger (1988) conceives of intentionality as the "comportemental structure of Dasein's behaviour" (p. 65). From this follows that knowledge and action are two sides of the same coin because it is through Dasein's existential comportment (care) that the being of the world can come to be disclosed (Sartre, 1991, p. 407).

Due to Dasein's care, the world appears as "presence-to-hand" and "readiness to hand" (Dreyfuss, 1995, p. xi). Presence-to-hand is in fact the phenomenon of presence-making or what Heidegger refers to as the "positedness of a thing" (Heidegger & Boss, 2001, p. 7). However, Heidegger claims that this has nothing to do with subjectivity; instead, positing is the application of an existing understanding to what is in front of us. For example, we immediately know an object is a garden bench when we see a bench in the garden because the necessary references are already available. In contrast, the readiness to hand phenomenon refers to a specific being revealed through our engagement with objects. For example, only by sitting on the bench in the garden can we understand that the garden bench is a useful being for my relaxation activities. Thus, Heidegger (2010) stated, "Beings are discovered with regard to the fact that they are referred as those beings which they are to something. They are relevant together with something else" (p. 82).

The key term is *discovered* because it reveals that Heidegger does not think that knowledge about the world is constituted in a synthesis of perception and apperception, but that knowledge is already resting in the world to being with. In other words, Dasein can only disclose Being from already existing perspectives, norms, and traditions and in a language that does not belong exclusively to the subject, but to everyone and no one. Hence, it is not an "ego" that constitutes what things are. Their Beings are already disclosed by "the dictatorship" of "the they" (Das Man; p. 123), and consequently, Dasein can only disclose its understanding of what is already understood by the they. Thus, Heidegger (2010) stated, we enjoy, ourselves and have fun the way *they* enjoy themselves. We read, see, and judge literature and art the way *they* see and judge. But we also withdraw from the "great mass" the way *they* withdraw, we find "shocking" what *they* find shocking. The they, which is nothing definite and which all are, though not as a sum, prescribes the kind of being of everydayness.

(p. 123)

Thus, in its concern or care for the world, Dasein falls prey to the mundane averageness of everydayness (Warren, 2014, p. 197).

In this manner, Heidegger solves the problem that Husserl (1973a) grappled with (i.e., "How can the pure phenomenon of cognition reach something which is not immanent to it?") (p. 5) by dismantling the Cartesian worldview with the insight that there is no actual delimitation between Dasein and world. Thus, Heidegger (2010) argued that "the they" or "Das Man" is a form of historical normative averageness that determines what Dasein can possibly come to understand about Being and its own possibilities of becoming. Das Man is publicness, and in Heidegger's view, "publicness initially controls every way in which the world and Dasein are interpreted" (p. 123).

The Phenomena of Free Will and Being-for-Itself

From Husserl's lectures on time consciousness, Sartre (2001) concluded that Husserl is correct that experience must be a synthesis of past and present consciousness. However, Sartre found that the significance of this insight is that "consciousness refers perpetually to itself" (p. 39). Sartre (2001) therefore concluded that for consciousness to be conscious of something, it first must be "conscious of itself" (p. 40). Merleau-Ponty (1978, p. ix) expressed this insight in the following manner: "I could not possibly apprehend anything as existing unless I first of all experienced myself as existing in the act of apprehending it." For example, Sartre (1992) stated, "[W]e cannot be conscious of this table by the window without being conscious of the fact that we are conscious" (p. 11), and in this manner, Sartre (1992) reconceptualizes consciousness as "self-consciousness" (p. 14).

Having established consciousness as a reflective self-consciousness, Sartre (1992) proceeded to formulate the following axiom: Consciousness "is a being such that in its being its being is in question" (p.120). Who is questioning, one may ask? The answer is that consciousness itself is questioning what it is and in answering, what Heidegger (2010, p. 262) refers to as the silent call of consciousness,

consciousness constitutes itself as the phenomenon of a being-for-itself. Thus, Sartre (1992) concluded that the human being is a "Being which determines itself to exist" (p.126) and therefore "man is nothing other than what he makes of himself" (Sartre, 2007, p. 22).

From this follows that freedom of choice is an existential condition and that the Being of the human being is constituted in every choice and decision we make (Sartre, 1992, p. 120). In addition, Sartre (1992) concluded that the world also reveals itself "across our conduct" (p. 614), which means that not only can the human being define itself (Sartre, 2007, p. 22), but we also choose the reality we live (Sartre, 1992, p. 616). Thus Sartre (1992) stated,

> [T]here are no accidents in life; a community event which suddenly bursts forth and involves me in it does not come from the outside. If I am mobilized in a war, this war is *my* war; it is in my image, and I deserve it. I deserve it first because I could always get out of it by suicide or dessertation (p. 708) and consequently concluded, any way you look at it, it is a matter of a choice.
>
> (p. 708)

From this perspective, we are not just subjects to the dictatorship of "Das Man" or constituting intentionalities. On the contrary, Sartre argued that we ultimately want to be God with the ability to shape the lifeworld in accordance with our own desires (Spiegelberg, 1971, p. 471). In other words, our selfness and by association the reality in which we live are correlates of free will. However, the peculiar in Sartre's analysis is the revelation that the experience of reality is constituted by intending something that does not yet exist. In other words, it is a desire for a future state of affairs that gives meaning to the present situation and in fact also determines the experience of the past as a road leading toward the end goal of our ambitions. Hence, Sartre (1992) stated, "The world itself is revealed in the light of the end" (p. 617). Consequently, Sartre (1992) argued that human reality should be conceived as a "rupture with the given" (p. 615) rather than a correlate of its objectification.

The Phenomena of Emplotment and Identity

For Ricoeur (1994), Sartre's notion that we are the authors of our own situations is no longer an allegory but is to be taken literally when exploring the "hermeneutics of the self" (p. 297). Like Sartre, Ricoeur's starting point was Heidegger's (2010) axiom that the mode of Dasein is "care" (p. 347), and he agreed with Heidegger that the question of Being becomes readable in human action. Thus, Ricoeur (1994) argued that "if an ontology of selfhood is possible – this is in conjunction with a ground starting from which the self can be said to be acting" (p. 308). However, in contrast to Sartre, Ricoeur did not subscribe to the idea that it is the action in itself that constitutes the self. Instead, Ricoeur posited that it is Dasein's ability to disclose being that is constitutive of the self (Rae, 2010, p. 24).

Consequently, Ricoeur (1994) argued that language is the medium through which the individuals constitute themselves as persons because it is in "speech acts that the agent of action designates himself or herself as the one who is acting" (p. 17). In this connection, Heidegger (1968) points out that the etymology of the word persona is "the actor's mask through which his dramatic tale is sounded" (p. 62). Consequently, Ricoeur (1994) argued that there is no "non rhetorical naturalness of language. Language is figurative through and through" (p. 12). Thus, within the hermeneutic tradition, language is considered a "mediator between the being and the thinking" (De Faria Blanc, 2005, p. 43), and Fink (1995, p. 85) therefore designated speech as a constitutive act in its own right.

However, the peculiarity of speech is that disclosures in fact say very little about what happened in the past. Ricoeur (1994) pointed out that memories of past experiences seem to consist of "an unstable mixture of fabulations and actual experience" (p. 162). Ricoeur (1979) therefore argued that the function of disclosure is not to accurately recall information from the past, but to "construe a significant whole out of scattered events" and thereby "organize life retrospectively" (p. 24), which makes it possible for individuals to emplot themselves in a storyline (Ricoeur, 1994, p. 142) that helps them make sense of their lives and provides them with a tentative answer of who they are.

Therefore, the question of the hermeneutics of the self is implicitly an interpretation of "who speaks? Who acts? Who tells his or her stories?" (p. 297). From this perspective, we must conceive of speech acts as primarily referring to "the speakers themselves who refer in this way" (p. 43) rather than representing an experience of an actual situation. Consequently, Ricoeur (1994) argued that "the language of act and power have never ceased to underlie our hermeneutical phenomenology of the acting man" (p. 303). From this follows that the "narrative conception of personal identity" requires us to conceive of identity as a correlate of emplotment "where the character preserves throughout the story an identity correlative to that of the story itself" (p. 143).

The Phenomenon of Embodiment and Being-for-the-Other

In *Being and Nothingness*, Sartre explored a perspective on the constitution of selfhood that draws equally on the individual's self-consciousness and the gaze of other people. Although the individuals ultimately choose themselves and their lifeworld, Sartre (1992) argued that the self is not "without doors or windows" (p. 654). Thus, an individual's freedom to choose its own reality is in direct competition with other individuals' chosen realities and therefore the self cannot insulate from the affect of other people (Spiegelberg, 1971, p. 470).

For example, when we are thrown into a conflict with other people, our primary experience is of this situation. In other words, our lived experience is not divided into two consecutive moments where we first sense our bodies and then this situation. Although our bodies are present in this conflict, we do not directly experience them as immanent to it.

What we perceive is how other people evaluate our bodily presence in this conflict (Moran, 2010, p. 52), and we, therefore, come to apperceive our bodies and this conflict as a synthetic totality (Sartre, 1992, p. 455). From this follows that our embodied selves are partly fully constituted from the affection of other people. Sartre (1992) named this phenomenon "the third ontological dimension of the body" (p. 460).

Hence, the constitution of our embodied selves is paradoxical because our egos are simultaneously inside and outside of us as we posit our selfness both as a being-for-itself and a being-for-others. Thus Sartre stated, "[W]ith the appearance of the other's look I experience the revelation of my being-as-object" (p. 461) and concluded that the "being-for-others haunts me" (p. 462). By this, he meant that the gaze of the other deprived him of control over his own body image or schema (Moran, 2010, p. 45). Consequently, the third ontological dimension of the body becomes an arena where the social power structures that critical phenomenology is concerned with battle it out for control of the embodied self.

In this manner, the conflict between "being for-it-self" and "being-for-the-other" became the point of departure for feminist and Black existentialists who took phenomenology in a new direction by critically examining the constitution of gendered and racialized selfhood within a patriarchal White society.

The Phenomenon: Being-for-the-Other and Woman

Simone de Beauvoir made the phenomenon of being a woman the theme of her seminal work *The Second Sex*, published in 1949, where she argued that one may be born female, but woman is something that one becomes. By this, she did not mean that woman or genders are social constructs, but that the power structures of the social and cultural environment play a role in how females constitute themselves as women in a precarious synthesis of being-for-itself and being-for-the-other. Thus, she argued that not every female is necessarily a woman because becoming a woman is a response to a situation that a female finds herself in and not a biological destination (de Beauvior, 2015, p. 4).

Here we can see a clear parallel to Sartre's (1992) insight regarding the synthetic unity of embodied selves and situations (p. 455), and consequently, we need to understand the situation females are in to understand how women become. In this way, de Beauvior (2015) pointed to the fact that, at least in her time, most females were power-less to choose their own situation. Therefore, the drama of becoming a woman lies in the conflict between the existential necessity that all individuals, male or female, posit themselves as essential, and "the demands of a situation that constitutes her as inessential" (p. 24). In other words, females find themselves in a situation where being a man has become the norm for being human and they, therefore, end up constituting themselves as women relative to men (p. 7), while the opposite is never the case. Thus, being a woman is not entirely a corre-late of a female's own choice and free will, but as much a correlate of the objectifying male gaze, which the female nevertheless chooses to internalize, and de Beauvoir, therefore, argued that women are com-plicit in constituting their own otherness (p. 13).

The Phenomenon of Nonbeing and Blackness

Blackness formally refers to skin color, and Alcoff (1999) explained that the concept of race originated in an early Eurocentric scientific project aimed at understanding nature by classifying objects into cate-gories and hierarchies. However, in the same way that early astrono-mers placed the earth at the center of the universe, White Europeans placed themselves at the top of the racial hierarchy. This constructed "natural order" provided the logic that ultimately justified centuries of colonialism and oppression.

In this manner, the lived reality of race is the synthesis of situation, body, and the gaze of the "other," which in White majority societies has the epistemic effect of constituting what Blackness is as a value, but in a way that makes it near impossible for a Black person to self-constitute in an authentic manner. While White females are in the difficult situation of having to strike a balance between being-for-itself and being-for-the-other, Frantz Fanon (2008) argued that the Black man is unable to constitute himself as a for-it-self. Thus, in his seminal work *Black Skin White Masks*, first published in 1952, Fanon (2008) argued that "ontology does not allow us to understand the being of the black man, since it ignores the lived experience. For not only must the black man be black; he must be black in relation to the white man" and therefore "in the white world the man of color encounters difficulties in elaborating his body schema" (p. 90).

Thus, White society relegates the Black person to what Fanon (2008) called "a zone of nonbeing" (p. xii), where Black people are not human beings but problems. For example, Collins (2020a) argued that even a well-meaning White person in America "sees Blackness as the damage it did to us, not the joy we take in ourselves." This is particularly evident if we consider the euphemisms for Black that are used in the social sciences: Underserved, inner city, marginalized, and under-banked populations. These euphemisms objectify Black people in terms of what White researchers conceive as being problematic. An alternative conceptualization could instead begin with potentials. For example, we readily refer to projects as being "shovel-ready" and not unbuilt.

4 I Think Therefore I Am

What we could call the "empirical subject" is the focus of naturalistic research. However, this kind of scientific research only contends with the physical *subject that is* but never really relates to *what that subject is*. Thus, in its commitment to objectivism, natural sciences take the subject for granted. The world is simply there to measure, and the subject is just another object in that world. Thus, Merleau-Ponty (Edie, 2000) critiqued the conceptualization of the human subject in psychological research as a simple collection of random traits that are chosen merely "because of their frequent occurrence" (p. 63) but "with no power to reveal the essence that must be understood" (p. 63). In addition, he found the conceptualization of the phenomenon of the human being "vague, confused and in need of psychological clarification" (Edie, 2000, p. 63). Therefore, to make human subject research possible, we need to theoretically demonstrate what we mean when we say human being. The question at stake is what Luft (2005, p. 142) referred to as the question of "a phenomenological anthropology."

The Transcendental Ego

Descartes (1911) came to see that the fact that he was doubting was beyond any doubt, and he, therefore, concluded that his essence was "a thing which thinks" (p. 10) and thus stated, "**I see clearly that there is nothing which is easier for me to know than my mind**" (p. 12) and coined the famous axiom "I think therefore I am."

Thus inspired, Husserl came to the insight that the ego has two dimensions. On one hand, we have a psychological ego who is living life in the world among other people (2017, p. 13) and takes the world

DOI: 10.4324/9781003270058-4

and its own status in the world for granted. However, when we apply the phenomenological reduction, we encounter another layer, where we find the transcendental ego, who according to Sartre (2001, p. 37) is "a necessary structure of consciousness whose rays (Ichstrahlen) would light upon each phenomenon presenting itself in the field of attention."

The transcendental ego is not a real personality, and Husserl (2017) explained that it is essentially empty; "it has no content that would be unraveled, it is in for itself indescribable: pure ego and nothing further" (p. 233). The transcendental ego is of course the same as the psychological ego, but Husserl (2017) argued that, due to the researcher's enactment of the epoché and reduction, the psychological ego "loses just that which makes it something real in the world that lies before us, it loses the meaning of the soul as belonging to a body that exists in an objective, spatial temporal nature" (p. 14). Hence in the reduction, the transcendental ego only appears as an "adjunct" (p. 234) of the intentional act and can therefore not be investigated empirically.

The Embodied Ego

While Husserl's conceptualization of the transcendental subject ends up being independent of both world and body, Merleau-Ponty's analysis in *Phenomenology of Perception* gives rise to some contention on this matter. Merleau-Ponty was probably the only phenomenological philosopher who followed psychological research, and through his investigation of perception, he came to doubt that the reduction could be completed beyond the body and consequently reconceptualized the transcendental subject as the pre-reflective living body (Pollard, 2014).

From this perspective, the body is not a container for the mind, but a plenum for human time consciousness. For example, Merleau-Ponty (1978) argued that the blushing of cheeks when remembering past embarrassments and the heart palpitations in anticipation of possible threats demonstrates the body's ability to manifest into the present "time past and time to come" (p. 69). Consequently, the body is not only "the seat of the five senses" (Sartre, 1992, p. 422) nor a mediator or "a screen between things and ourselves" (p. 428). The body is a "field of perception and action" (Edie, 2000, p. 16), where body language reflects the lived world but at the same time turns around and signifies the meaning of the situations we find ourselves in.

The Psychological Ego

In phenomenological research, the subject is not just a thing with biological and demographic characteristics because the phenomenologist posits the subject as a "knowing subject" (Thompson & Zahavi, 2007) and not an object in the world. By this, we mean that the world is there for the psychological ego, and, in contrast to the transcendental ego, we cannot conceive of an "experiential self" "independently of its connection with the world" (Sousa, 2014, p. 42).

Within the phenomenological tradition, there is a tendency to be overtly analytical, and some scholars conceptualize the ego as little more than a unifying principle between the lived experience and the world (Sartre, 2001, p. 31). For example, Fink (1995, p. lii) concluded that in the final analysis, the phenomenon of the human being is the natural attitude itself. In contrast, proponents of genetic phenomenology conceive time consciousness as the "basis of selfhood" (Sousa, 2014, p. 38), where the ego constitutes of itself from what has happened to it and what it strives to become. Consequently, in genetic phenomenology, the individual's self-temporalization becomes the theme of analysis, where the researcher can look at either the formation of identity (Sousa, 2014, p. 37) or at how the lifeworld organizes around the structures of the ego's personal life (Husserl, 1970, p. 328).

The They-Self and Dasein

Heidegger argued that to understand Dasein, we must abandon the idea of an interior subjectivity and an exterior reality. This was clearly expressed in the transcripts from the Zollikon seminars, where Heidegger stated,

> In the perspective of the Analytic of Da-sein, all conventional, objectifying representations of a capsule like psyche, subject, person, ego or consciousness in psychology and psychopathology must be abandoned in favour of an entirely different understanding. This new view of the basic constitution of human existence may be called *Da-sein*, or being-in-the-world.
>
> (Heidegger & Boss, 2001, p. 4)

From this follows that Dasein does not perceive or reflect, but handles and takes care of things (Luft, 2005, p. 145), and therefore Dasein can best be described as a "happening" (Dreyfus, 1995, p. 163). Thus

Merleau-Ponty (1978) argued, "[T]ruth does not inhabit only the inner man or more accurately, there is no inner man, man is in the world and only in the world does he know himself" (p. xi). For example, the writer becomes a writer because he writes. Writing is a form of relating that simultaneously discloses both the Being of the writer's world and the writer's own Being. Thus, Heidegger (1988) argued that "to the Dasein there belongs essentially a disclosed world and with that the disclosedness of the Dasein itself" (18).

We can therefore say that Dasein loses itself to the world when it discloses it. For example, the writer writes in a style that may be unique to him or her, but there still is a silent transcendence of themes that announces some Being already grasped prior to putting pen on paper, and therefore the writer just interprets what is already tacitly understood by "Das Man." In this manner, the world is not "a matter of private experiences" (Dreyfus, p. 145). Instead, Dasein is essentially a publicness "dispersed in the they." Therefore, Dasein is not an authentic self but should be understood as a "they-self" (Heidegger, 2010, p. 125). Thus Heidegger (2010) argued that Das Man or "the they" "disburdens Dasein in its everydayness" from coming face-to-face with its own authentic self. Hence, "the 'they' is the nobody whom the everyday Dasein has always surrendered itself" (p. 124).

The Self

In contrast to Husserl, Sartre (2001) found that there is no ego inside the lived experience (Erlebnis) and in general that "there is no I at the unreflected level" (p. 48) of consciousness. There is only consciousness of objects and situations (p. 49), and the ego first appears as a transcendence from the reflective act (p. 53). In other words, the idea of a "myself" first appears as a "concrete type of existence" (p. 52) when the individual reflects on the project of living and the desired state of affairs of life. Therefore, Sartre (1992) likened consciousness to "a plenum of existence" (p. 16), where consciousness determines its own being in the sense that our choices and actions "returns upon the ego" (p. 82) and qualify it.

Hence, Sartre (1992) argued that "the ego is not the owner of consciousness" (p. 97) as we would find it to be the case within phenomenological psychology. On the contrary, it is consciousness that "under certain conditions allows the appearance of the ego as the transcendent phenomenon" (p. 156) of consciousness's self-reflection.

The Narrative Self

In contrast to Sartre's self-consciousness, the narrative self does not will itself into existence but recognizes itself by communicating and interacting with others (Ricoeur, 1994, p. 329). Thun (2010) therefore argued that language is similar to art as a symbolic way to ourselves (p. 342). In this connection, Heidegger (2001b) pointed out that speech is not merely a faculty, but that which "enables man to be the living being he is as man" (p. 187). By this, he meant that speech is not mere language; it is also an act by which the "I" constitutes its identity by transforming experiences into narratives with a plot. Thus, Ricoeur (1994) argued that "the plot is placed in the service of the character" (p.148) and not the other way around. In this manner, a person's identity becomes a correlative of its own emplotment, and, consequently, there is no distinction between plot and a person's identity (p. 148).

The Embodied Self

The embodied self has the same constitutive agency as the psychological subject but is unable to exercise this in a sovereign manner. The problem is that the self is not able to fully perceive its own body. Thus, Sartre (1992) argued that "the body is lived and not known" (p. 427). By this, Sartre meant that we apperceive our own embodiment from the situations in which we find ourselves (Edie, 2000, p. 51), where we encounter what other bodies look like and experience how other embodied subjects respond to our presence (Moran, 2010, p. 44). Consequently, Sartre (1992) concluded, "I see myself because somebody sees me" (p. 349) and thereby our embodied selves cease to be empirical beings. Instead, our presence is transformed into a symbol or a value that is contingent on the gaze of others rather than our own agency.

Female Consciousness

Female is a predicated object defined by biological traits and therefore falls under the domain of natural science. Thus, de Beauvoir pointed out that one is not born woman, but it is something that one becomes through the situations females must respond to. The problem is that due to the well-documented patriarchal power structures, females have historically been unable to choose their own situations.

This fact has reinforced the belief that females are less capable of coping with said situations, although they were not the author of those to begin with. Hence, the otherness of women is derived from a perceived helplessness as well as being recipients of male benevolence and sexual interest. Thus, de Beauvior (2015, p. 24) argued that becoming woman happens in the conflict between being-for-itself and being-for-others. Along these lines, Kaplan (1982) argued that female consciousness is an acquired state of mind where the gender system of society is simply accepted. Being a woman is fulfilling the role of caregiver and spouse and of the roles that are assigned to them more so than demanding the rights that these obligations entail (p. 545). Sartre (1992) referred to this form of consciousness as "bad faith," and by this he meant an inclination to deny the qualities that one naturally possesses and stated, "to not seeing the being which I am" (p. 111).

Although de Beauvoir's insights resonate, her conceptualization of woman has been criticized for expressing the perspective of White middle-class women and ignoring the intersectionality of "race, class, ethnic, national and sexual identities" (Bergoffen, 2018, p. 331), and the notion of patriarchal dominance ignores the fact that "white women have had power over minority women and men" (p. 331).

The Double or Triple Consciousness of the Black Person

Heidegger (2002) argued that the essence of identity "stems from that letting belong together which we call appropriation." However, for the Black person, White society interrupts this event because it projects a range of negative values back on the Black person and makes them feel consistently alien and unwelcome in social situations, which ultimately are not of their own choosing. Thus, Du Bois (1994) argued that Black people struggle to achieve true self-consciousness because they always look at themselves through the eyes of the White majority. He referred to this constitutional limbo, where the Black person is measuring themselves "by the tape of a world that look on in amused contempt and pity" (p. 8), as a state of having a "double-consciousness" (p. 8).

This concept has been thoroughly elaborated on and should be considered a theoretical position rather than an actual condition. In this way, Fanon's *Black Skin White Masks* is a work illustrative of the Black person's difficulties in navigating White colonial society and appropriating his Being in an authentic manner. On the other hand, Fanon's book is also a testimony to a person who is thoroughly at home in their own skin and Being as they seemingly reject the binary choice that double consciousness presents in favor of the whole human being.

Nevertheless, these historical conceptualizations of Black selfhood can rightly be criticized for ignoring the plight of Black women. Thus, Welang (2018) argued that Black American women are caught between "white patriarchy and black hypermasculinity" (p. 296), where even in Black spaces, Black female voices are oppressed and likewise shunned in the feminist movement led by White women. Welang (2018) therefore proceeded to formulate a "triple consciousness theory" (p. 296), where the Black woman apperceives herself from three perspectives: (a) the White patriarchy, (b) the Black hypermasculine patriarchy, and (c) a feminism that "prioritizes the interests of white women" (p. 305).

5 Why Are We Studying First-Person Point of View Experiences?

The scientific method has yielded tremendous technological progress and assisted us in formulating observation-based laws of cause and effect pertaining to our natural environment and our bodies. In a similar manner, psychology has tried to rid itself of its speculative origin by embracing the scientific method (Gantt & Williams, 2020). Although the 19th century witnessed the triumph of science, Husserl nevertheless proclaimed that the human sciences were in a crisis (Hanna, 2014, p. 753). The reason is that naturalistic metaphysics, which underpins the scientific method, is committed to the assumption that reality can be observed and measured, and that empirical observation has the power to distinguish what is real and what is not.

However, for the scientific method to work, the researcher must operationalize phenomena into observable variables, and they thereby limit their research to only "the outward manifestation of the phenomenon" (Gant & Williams, 2019, p. 89). For example, Eagly and Chaiken (1993), in their seminal work *The Psychology of Attitude*, posited that "an individual does not have an attitude until he or she responds evaluatively to an entity" (p. 2). Further, they posited that these entities are "encoded from a variety of stimuli" that when "observed elicit responses expressing a certain degree of evaluation" (p. 5). They exemplified this by "the attitude object my brother" (p. 5), which is encoded with the following stimuli, "his name, a picture of him, a letter from him etc." (p. 5), and concluded that when "the classes of stimuli that denote my brother are observed" (p. 5), they produce an evaluative response that infers a certain attitude. In fact, they claimed that if a statistically significant evaluative tendency can be observed, then researchers can infer an attitude (p. 2).

However, Eagly and Chaiken (1993) ran into the problem of construct validity because it is not entirely obvious how a statistical

DOI: 10.4324/9781003270058-5

measure of evaluative tendency can infer a subjective psychological phenomenon such as an attitude. Thus, Eagly and Chaiken's attitude construct falls prey to scientific operationalism because their move to displace the attitude phenomenon with a tendency is only convenient for statistical analysis.

In other words, evaluative tendencies are false psychological facts about attitudes, and by false I do not mean to say that there is no connection between the exterior world and the mental realm, but rather that facts produced about such connections "are not the real facts-of-the-matter of the phenomenon" (Gantt & Williams, 2020, p. 89) because we have learned nothing about how attitudes are lived through time and space. Consequently, statistical measures have no ontological value for understanding what an attitude is (Edie, 2000, p. 57).

While it is correct that our minds are impacted by the world, empirical psychology ignores that the subject is at the same time positing this very same world as an "intentional object" (Edie, 2000, p. 57). Fink (1995, p. 35) therefore stated that there is "no other world than the one experienced in my experiences, the one meant in my beliefs" and consequently that "human life in the world is a belief-construct."

Hence, it was an objectivist fallacy when Eagly and Chaiken (1993) postulated that a person does not have an attitude before "he or she responds evaluatively to an entity" (p. 2). Thus, Husserl argued that assumed casual connections do not represent the experience, and neither are they experienced (Husserl, 1977, p. 4). In this way, Sartre (1992) argued that "there is an infinite number of realities which are not only objects of judgment, but which are experienced ... by human beings and which in their inner structure are inhabited by negation" (p. 55).

To illustrate his point, Sartre (1992) told a story of going to meet his friend Pierre in a busy café, but when Sartre arrived, Pierre was not there, and because Sartre expected him to be there, Sartre's experience of the café can be summed up by the following exclamation: "Pierre absent haunts this café" (p. 42). Thus, Sartre stated that "I myself expected to see Pierre, and my expectations has caused the absence of Pierre to happen as a real event concerning this café" (p. 42). In other words, Sartre's elaboration on nothingness demonstrated that while nothingness has no actual existence and therefore cannot be operationalized for empirical research, it is evident that, in the words of Sartre (1992), "my establishment of Pierre's absence could still be determinant for my regret of not seeing him" (p. 63).

The Copenhagen Interpretation

The constitutive role of consciousness is largely ignored in modern psychology, and the reason consciousness and spirit have largely been exiled from research can be found in the Newtonian worldview, which posited a mechanistic universe governed by the laws of cause and effect. Consequently, consciousness endured a functionalistic reinterpretation as simple being the consequences of the input the mind receives from an exterior world. Thus, modern science and social research came to embrace the assumption that reality exists objectively, independently from the cognizant process of empirical verification (Heisenberg, 2007, p. 56).

Schrödinger (2019) thus stated,

> So we are faced with the following remarkable situation. While the stuff from which our world picture is built is yielded exclusively from the sense organs as organs of the mind, so that every man's world picture is and always remains a construct of his mind and cannot be proved to have any other existence, yet the conscious mind itself remains a stranger within that construct, it has no living space in it, you can spot it nowhere in space.
>
> (p. 122)

Nevertheless, with the advent of the Copenhagen interpretation of quantum theory, the universal validity of the separation between the world and the subject has once again been brought into question (Heisenberg, 2007, p. 55). For example, Heisenberg (2007) noted that in the process of observing the behavior of particles, it would appear that "observations play a decisive role in the event and that the reality varies depending upon whether we observe it or not" (p. 26). Consequently, quantum experiments have demonstrated that objectification is not fully possible since subjectivity constitutes the state of measurements (Proietti et al., 2019) and Schrödinger (2019) therefore concluded that "the transition from possible to actual takes place during the act of observation" (p. 28), and from the natural standpoint of the human observer, this moment is also conceived as the beginning of a forward moving timeline (p. 147).

Thus, Schrödinger (2019, p. 93) posited that when we experience the world

> it is convenient to regard it as existing objectively on its own. But it certainly does not become manifest by its mere existence. It's becoming manifest is conditional on very special goings-on in

very special parts of this very world, namely on certain events that happen in a brain.

Consequently, Schrödinger (2019) argued that

> we cannot make any factual statement about a given natural object (of physical system) without getting in touch with it. This "touch" is a real physical interaction. Even if it consists only in our looking at the object the latter must be hit by light-rays and reflect them into the eye, or into some instrument of observation. This means that the object is affected by our observation. You cannot obtain any knowledge about an object while leaving it strictly isolated.
>
> (p. 125)

This is what is often referred to as the observer effect, but it does not mean that there is a causality between the particles and the observer nor that the observer causes time to be set in motion. Instead, the observer effect implies that "what we observe is not nature itself, but nature exposed to our method of questioning" (Heisenberg, 2007, p. 32). Further, the observer effect implies that human conception of time originates from our conceptions of a cause and effect, which in perception is just a change of status from a before to an after state (Schrödinger, 2019, p. 147).

Here we have a remarkable parallelism between quantum theory and phenomenological theory, where on the one hand Heidegger concluded that natural science is mistaken to view the relationship between the human being and the world as the relationship between two extant objects because subjectivity and objectivity are just opposite poles on the same existential continuum. Thus, Heisenberg (2007, p. 55) cautioned that we must avoid the fallacy of the scientific method that implicitly assumes that it is possible to empirically describe the world without referring to the subject. Conrad-Martius, therefore, argued, "There is a strong sense in which the entire cosmos is radically spiritual" (Hart, 2020, p. 162) and that the purpose of real ontology is to grasp the logos that constitutes what we experience as a completed reality.

Temporality and Epistemological Phenomenology

Giorgi (2019) warned, "when psychology explicitly sets out to imitate natural scientific methodology, it never realizes that it implicitly also accepted the assumptions underlying the methodology" (p. 54). These assumptions are what we call "logos," and when this word shows up at the end of method (i.e., method-ology), we are made aware that we are about to accept a certain theoretical perspective on reality. Thus, when we use an observation-based scientific methodology, we implicitly also accept metaphysical naturalism and the perspective on reality we call nature. Heidegger, (2014) explained that in Latin "natura" means "birth" (p. 15), and this perspective compels us to narrow our investigation of what is real "in the direction of the physical" (p. 18). Hence, the logos of metaphysical naturalism dictates that observational methods have the power to determine the truth about what things are.

In contrast, Heidegger (2014) pointed out that there is a difference between the metaphysical question about "beings as such" and the philosophical question about "Being as such" (p. 21). The distinction made by his use of a capitol "B" indicates that we are here asking thematically about the Being of beings, which he argued, "does not consist in our observing beings" (p. 37). In this connection, Conrad-Martius posited that the world is not just in a container that we can look into and apprehend its content. Instead, we must understand that space-time is "the mode of being of the world" (Hart, 2020, p. 237), and therefore phenomenology is not just an eidetic analysis of perceptions or comportment, but "the disclosure of the Logos of what shows itself" (p. 236).

Similarly, Husserl (1977) argued that "a psychology which foregoes grounding what happens in the mind upon the intelligible nexus of mental life is necessarily untruthful" (p. 9). With this statement, Husserl indicated that the truth is essentially apodictic and not empirical. Thus, Tymeinecka (2006) concluded that the logos that orders the Being of beings thematically is "temporality" (p. xxxiii), where "consciousness in its flow of acts becomes a processor" of temporality and thereby makes it possible for the meaning of the world to "come together into an apperceptive glance" (p. xxx). Therefore, investigation of the first-person point of view is necessary not only for the purpose of elucidating individuals' experiences but also to understand thematically what it means for something to Be.

From our earlier elaborations on time consciousness, we have a clear indication that time is somehow part of the fabric of experiences and constitutive of the Being of beings. This insight led the mature Husserl to move away from a static toward a more genetic perspective on phenomenology. Hence, the act of perception is not only a static case of giving reality to cognition. Perception can also be conceived as a dynamic phenomenon (i.e., "the point of authentic perceiving to which a continuous sequence of retentions is joined" [Husserl, 2019, p. 100]). For example, the most common way we encounter tones is from musical compositions. This example reveals that for us to make the distinction between one tone and another, an a priori notion of before and after must be a feature of our experience horizon (Husserl, 2019, p. 23). Thus, the experience of a melody requires that past tones retain their salience in the perception of the tone in the now-point, while at the same time, the perception must include anticipation of the next plausible note. If this were not the case, how would we ever know if someone sings off-key? This conceptualization implies that the perceptions are constituted by time consciousness and that perceived "objects" are not only physical representations but also "temporal beings" (Husserl, 2019, p. 101).

Temporality and Existential Phenomenology

On the other side of the phenomenological schism, Heidegger rejected the constitutive role of subjectivity, but that does not mean that temporality is no longer in play, just that it is no longer a structure of intentionality. Thus, Heidegger (1988) argued that "Dasein understands the interpretation of Being is connected in some form or other with time" (p. 303) and that it is Dasein's historical understanding of what Being is that provides Dasein with possibilities to care about things and situations in certain ways (Koloskov, 2022).

Fink (1995) argued that the creation of knowledge about what things are is the accomplishment of a "historico-generative communication" (p. 105). From this perspective, building knowledge is contingent on acts of communication and not procedure. The question of Being, therefore, becomes a thematic question about Dasein's historical comportment to beings (Heidegger, 2014, p. 49). In this manner, Dasein's care about what is ready-to-hand in the world not only discloses the Being of beings but reveals that Being is temporal (Warren, 2014, p. 195). Heidegger (1988) therefore argued that time is the "transcendental horizon" (p. 323) that allows our analysis of what things are to move from being as such to Being as such.

For example, when Dasein encounters a situation or an object, it is not the case that time consciousness and apperception build up an idea of what this situation or object is. Dasein is historical and therefore already aware of a wide range of possibilities for Being. It is therefore Dasein's projection of these temporal possibilities upon situations and things, which allows Dasein to objectify them and to accomplish their "conceptualizability" (Heidegger, 1988, p. 323). Thus Heidegger (1988) posited that in the final analysis, "all propositions of ontology are temporal propositions" (p. 323) "about being in the light of time" (p. 324).

However, Sartre (1992, p. 62) argued that a temporal interpretation of the Being of beings is too narrow if we only conceive of temporality in terms of a retention of the past. Thus, Sartre suggested that a given situation is "appreciated in terms of something which does not yet exist," (p. 615). In other words, we care for things in the "now" not because of the past, but for the possibility of a desired future state of affairs. Consequently, Sartre (1992) argued that the past "is without force to constitute the present" (p. 637) and that "man is before all else, something that projects itself into a future" (Sartre, 2007, p. 23).

In summary, the first-person point of view has priority in phenomenological research because no science can go beyond the experience horizon of the human being. Thus, Husserl (1970) stated that phenomenology is an attempt at understanding how objectivity is constituted, and therefore the purpose of the phenomenological method is not "to secure objectivity but to understand it" (p. 189).

The question is whether the researcher conceives of temporality as constitutive of the intentional acts or whether temporality primarily is an interpretative horizon. However, these are perspectives that are often absent in applied phenomenological studies. Consequently, phenomenological analyses often appear static as they tend to conceive of experiences as various now-points instead of temporal accomplishments. Thus, without due consideration of temporality, the researcher may struggle to produce genuine phenomenological insights (Warren, 2014).

6 Epistemological Phenomenology

Epistemological phenomenology is a term that loosely refers to the idea of a knowing subject, whose capacity to experience is directed toward something. Thus, Husserl (2017) argued "to have something in mind is the cardinal feature of all consciousness" (p. 262), and we refer to this "directedness" as the phenomenon of intentionality.

In Husserl's early days, he attempted to develop a psychological theory of pure logic by studying "the psychological acts that give rise to logical concepts" (Kockelmans & Jager 1967, p. 87). Initially, Husserl referred to his philosophical project as descriptive psychology, as he believed that the concepts of pure logic could be observed by examining subjective experiences (p. 90). However, Husserl gradually became disenchanted with the limitations of descriptive psychology because it limited his investigations of logic to the natural standpoint, and this would hardly suffice considering his ambitious statement that "the sole task and service of phenomenology is to clarify the meaning of this world" (2017, p. 21).

Transcendental phenomenology and phenomenological psychology are in fact two sides of the same coin and just two different ways of understanding the thinking ego. Thus Husserl (2017) argued, "We have thus a remarkable thoroughgoing parallelism between a (properly elaborated) phenomenological psychology and a transcendental phenomenology" (p. 15). Hence, phenomenological psychology considers how the psychological ego takes possession of objects and situations and posits its lifeworld. In contrast, transcendental phenomenology considers the transcendental ego's ideal objectification of reality that makes experience possible in the first place (Kockelmans & Jager 1967, p. 123). Obviously, the transcendental realm is beyond the reach of empirical research; however, a basic understanding of transcendental subjectivity is necessary to provide a theoretical and methodological frame of reference for phenomenological psychology (see Luft, 2004a, p. 88).

DOI: 10.4324/9781003270058-6

The presentation of phenomenological psychology will be some-what different than what readers of Giorgi's work are accustomed to since the emphasis will be on the foundational literature from Husserl's later genetic phase. Thus, genetic phenomenology articulates the problem of constitution from the theoretical perspective of time consciousness rather than static subjectivity. Consequently, this book will introduce a version of phenomenological psychology that is both descriptive and explanatory.

Transcendental Phenomenology

Husserl (2017) posited that it is only through the essential structures of consciousness "that the fact-world comes to be known" (p. 113). This led Husserl to proclaim a crisis of the natural sciences, and due to the limitations of the deductive methods, he concluded that especially the human sciences are confounding facts with knowledge (Husserl, 2017, p. 82). Thus Husserl (1970) argued

> that to deduce is not to explain. To predict, or to recognize the objective forms of the compositions of physical or chemical bodies and to predict accordingly – all this explains nothing but is in need of explanation. The only true way to explain is to make tran-scendentally understandable. Everything objective demands to be understood.
>
> (p. 189)

Husserl (2001a) therefore posited that "logical concepts, as valid thought-unities, must have their origin in intuition: they must arise out of an ideational intuition founded on certain experiences" (p. 88).

From a transcendental phenomenological perspective, the study of intentionality "excludes the natural performance of all empirical apperceptions and positing" (Husserl, 2001a, p. 95), and Husserl (2017) pointed out that where "psychology is a science of realities" (p. 44) and that the phenomena in phenomenological psychology research are based in real events, then "transcendental phenomenology will be established not as a science of facts, but as a science of essential being; a science which aims exclusively at establishing knowledge of essences and absolutely no facts" (p. 44). Consequently, Husserl's transcendental phenomenology is not in the business of studying phenomenal appearances of objects, but instead focused on "that in which the appearing of this object resides, the real content immanent to consciousness i.e., intentional acts" (Romano, 2012 p. 430).

To this end, Husserl tried to work out a range of methods hereunder the epoché and the phenomenological reduction and it is not entirely unfair to state that Husserlian phenomenology came to be defined as much by its methods as its objective. Thus, Husserl (1970, p. 70) referred to the epoché as the breakthrough method that would reconstitute modern philosophy as a discipline grounded in self-evident truths and thus stated, "[T]he disconnexion from Nature was for us the methodological means whereby the direction of the mental glance upon the pure transcendental consciousness become at all possible" (Husserl, 2017, p. 171).

The epoché appears counterintuitive because it seeks to suspend the natural standpoint (i.e., our normal understanding of the world and its causalities in order to redirect our attention to intentionality). From this reorientation, the phenomenologists enact the phenomenological reduction, which leads our reflections back toward the constitutive meaning horizon of first the psychological ego. Subsequently, they are reflected toward the transcendental ego where all phenomenal representations of real objects and situations are removed so that the ideal objectivity of intentional acts can be contemplated.

The phenomenological reduction presents the applied researcher with an insurmountable problem because (a) there is no empirical distinction between an appearance and the mode of appearing (Zahavi, 2019, p. 84); (b) to the extent that the essence is of a transcendental nature, these findings cannot be empirically verified nor triangulated; and (c) Husserl (2001a) pointed out it is virtually impossible to describe the objectivities of intentional acts "without using expressions which recur to the things to which such acts refer" (p. 91). Consequently, transcendental phenomenology is not empirical research, but a philosophical position that critiques and informs research by revealing the ideal form of objectification (i.e., essence).

While we are not able to empirically study transcendental subjectivity, we can apply Husserl's theories of constitution in a theoretical framework underpinning a phenomenological psychological study. Thus, the phenomenological psychologist can at any time push the eidetic reduction into a full-blown phenomenological reduction and experience the transcendental realm and thereby gain a broader frame of reference. Thus, Husserl (1970) explained that the psychologist would acquire

> all the new sorts of apperceptions which are exclusively tied to the phenomenological reduction; together with the new sort of language – all this, which before was complete hidden and

inexpressible, now flows into the self-objectification, into my psychical life, and becomes apperceived as its newly revealed intentional background of constitutive accomplishments.

(p. 210)

Phenomenology of Embodiment

Merleau-Ponty concurred with Husserl that there is a crisis in the human sciences because the scientific methods presuppose that all outcomes of psychological research must find their cause in external variables (Edie, 2000, p. 43). Thus, Merleau-Ponty (1978) pointed out that for modern science, "the living body became an exterior without interior, subjectivity became an interior without an exterior" (p. 56). Nevertheless, Merleau-Ponty et al. (1968) argued, "One does not see how a social psychology would be possible. ... If one really thinks that perception is a function of exterior variables, this schema is applicable only to the corporeal and physical conditioning" (p. 23). Hence, the purpose of Merleau-Ponty's seminal work *Phenomenology of Perception*, published in 1945 was "to pursue the analysis of this exceptional relation between the subject and its body and its world" (Edie, 2000, pp. 4–5).

Merleau-Ponty's *Phenomenology of Perception* provides its readers with dense and often tedious descriptions of psychosomatic phenomena. However, his many detailed examinations of body–mind phenomena have inspired a contemporary view on health care, where body, mind, and social circumstances are seen as a unity. Specifically, proponents of the biopsychosocial theory of health refer to Merleau-Ponty's *Phenomenology of Perception* as a source of inspiration (Bolton & Gillet, 2019, p. 79), and a recent paper (Stilwell & Harman, 2019) on pain demonstrates how the experience of pain cannot be reduced to causalities between a stimulus and the body's nervous system. Instead, pain is a relational phenomenon of the entire lived body and its relationship with challenges in the external world to which it adapts.

Merleau-Ponty (1978) also had a philosophical goal with *Phenomenology of Perception*: to establish a phenomenological theory of the embodied mind. Merleau-Ponty agreed with Husserl's critique of psychologism, where the mental is reduced to a simple consequence of conditioning and external stimuli, but he was also skeptical of Husserl's tendency toward logicism, where essence is oblivious to actual experiences (Edie, 2000, p. 51). Hence, Merleau-Ponty broke with Husserl by positing that intentionality is not only the mode of consciousness but a body-mediated engagement with reality.

Similarly, applied researchers often misconstrue the notion of perception as a particular point of view or a judgment. The problem with misconstruing perceptions as beliefs is that researchers lose sight of the actual goings on of the experience and consequently the role the embodied perception plays in constituting reality (Pollard, 2014). Thus, perception can best be understood as the constitutive backdrop of all reason because, in the final analysis, reason must ultimately be grounded in some form of unreflected experience. Consequently, perception is not just a state of mind but a world openness of the lived body.

In this manner, the body is conceived as a field of experience and expression with a double function. On one hand, the body manifests the environment in which it lives. For example, abject poverty or social stressors clearly manifest in the body's form and gestures. On the other hand, the state of our bodies and gestures also "turns back on the world to signify it" (Edie, 2000, p. 7).

For the applied researcher, the aforementioned insights imply that data from body language is as meaningful as words if not more in determining the meaning of the subject's lifeworld. The body reacts intuitively and authentically and therefore as a field of experience may be the closest thing to the lived experience a researcher can observe. Thus, Merleau-Ponty (1978, p. 185) reminds us that gestures are not symbolic, but a bodily intentionality that posits a certain object in a certain way. For example, when faced with angry gestures, Merleau-Ponty argued, "I do not see a psychic fact hidden behind the gesture, I read anger in it. The gesture does not make me think of anger, it is anger itself" (p. 184). Nevertheless, the research literature focusing solely on embodiment is limited. It is typically experimental or appears in the form of triangulation of interview data, where the researcher takes note of salient body language.

Phenomenological Psychology and Genesis Research

Initially, Husserl (1997, p. 34) did not have a particular interest in psychological research and saw the natural standpoint of the ego as a staging ground for access to the transcendental realm. Consequently, his examples of psychological thought experiments tended to be static rather than a fully worked-out phenomenological psychological program (Husserl, 1997, p. 34). For example, Husserl's (2017, p. 53) investigation into the meaning-essence of sound perception revealed that every sound has its own essential nature, but submitted to eidetic variation, the universal derivative of all sounds is acoustics. Thus, Husserl

(1977, p. 16) concluded that acoustics is an ideal object that no longer refers to any specific sound, but to all possible and conceivable sounds.

Kockelmans (1987) argued that Husserl's reason for expanding his phenomenological project into psychology was his realization that psychology lacked "a systematic framework of basic concepts grounded in the intuitive clarification of the psychical essences" (p. 6), which the previous example is an illustration of. However, the domain and research methods of phenomenological psychology remained relatively underdeveloped until the emergence of the Dutch School of phenomenological psychology (Bas & Van Manen, 2002, p. 276), which later spread to the United States with Duquesne University as its epicenter.

In this connection, Kockelmans and Jager (1967) suggested that phenomenological psychological research should occupy an important role in clarifying "the meaning and coherence of those aspects of the psychical that are measured and correlated" (p. 185) in deductive psychological research. Thus, Kockelmans (1987) stated that "phenomenological psychology is destined to supply the essential insights needed to give meaning and direction to the research presented under the title empirical psychology" (p. 6).

Further, Giorgi defined phenomenological psychology as the study of "meanings as lived and contextualized within the mundane, everyday lifeworld" (Englander & Morley, 2021). However, the purpose is not so much to understand the life world, but to "understand humans in the world in a psychological way" (Giorgi, 2009, p. 190). The paradigm, therefore, centers around the elucidation of the ontological content of established psychological concepts, such as jealousy (Giorgi, 2009), self-deception, and victimization (Giorgi, 1985), where the everyday lifeworld becomes a means to this end.

It is one thing to study the first-person point of view to clarify the meaning of conceptual thought, but it is an entirely different challenge to elucidate the facticity and genesis of the "meant." To this end, the discovery of time consciousness brings the constitutive power of human subjectivity into the view of the phenomenological researcher in a new way. Thus, we see a gradual evolution from the static and descriptive phenomenology found in Husserl's earlier work toward a more explanatory phenomenology where Husserl applies a temporal perspective that brings retention and memories into the constitutive process (Steinbock, 1998, p. 144).

Husserl's contemplation of time consciousness (Sousa, 2014, p. 32), his lectures known as the *Analyses Concerning Passive and Active Synthesis* (1920–25), and finally his last major work *Experience and*

Judgement, published in 1939, gave rise to what is known as genetic phenomenology. While static phenomenology is focused on describing how objects and situations correlate with subjectivity to present as meanings, then genetic phenomenology studies the genesis of meanings by illuminating the psychological facts that constitute the structure of experiencing (Bower, 2020, p. 189). In other words, genetic phenomenology takes aim at how consciousness arises out of our interest in the world around us (Alves, 2021, p. 209).

Husserl (1973b) acknowledged that none of the objects of his static thought experiments appeared on their own, but always together with something else and stated,

> It is not open to doubt that there is no experience of things, in the simple and primary sense of an experience of things, which, grasping a thing for the first time and bringing cognition to bear on it, does not already "know" more about the thing than is in this cognition alone.
>
> (p. 31)

In this connection, Scheler (1954) explained that meaning-giving acts would be "a complete shot in the dark" (p. 229) if there was not a "genetic order in our knowledge" (p. 219) that provides for the existence and value of what we encounter in advance. Hence, the experience is not a static constitutive accomplishment, but rather a temporal structure, where the ego actualizes experience in judgments built upon previous judgments retained in memory (Husserl, 2001b, p. 302). Thus Husserl argued, "[T]he original core of judgment's being, that of constitution, is a being in the mode of created being, that is, a being in the form of temporality" (2001b, p. 302). In other words, the objects and situations we experience as "types" do not just arrive as such but are constituted through a succession of apperceptions (Steinbock, 1998, p. 142).

Husserl did not reject the notion that intentional acts of consciousness such as perception serve as the constitutive backdrop of reason but acknowledged that, from the natural standpoint of the ego, experiences actualize in the higher order intentionality of judging (Drummond, 2003, p. 19). Thus, Husserl (1973b) argued that judgment is "the name for the totality of objectivating ego-acts" (p. 61) that constitute an experience as an experience "about-which" (p. 19), a type of experience and "what the existent is" (p. 19). Consequently, all "the categorical forms which constitutes the theme of formal ontology accrue to objects in the act of judgment" (p. 12).

As judgment takes place in the natural attitude rather than in the lived experience, genetic phenomenological research takes its starting point at the moment where the ego takes possession of its perception and constitutes the world as a certain state of affairs (Drummond, 2003, p. 84). Researchers will attempt to elucidate this "state of affairs in its relation to the genealogy of the judgement act" (Drummond, 2003, p. 84). They may achieve this by identifying and describing the constitutive role of "sedimented experiences" (Lohmar, 2014, p. 268), which is the surplus data derived from memory that the apperceiving ego adds to the perception. Thus Husserl (1973b) argued that "apperceptive transference" (p. 124) of analogous experiences posit phenomena as familiar types of phenomena through an act of judgment.

Thus, the genetic phenomenological research perspective "takes up an interpretive position with respect to the teleological genesis of sense" (Steinbock, 1998, p. 128), and in this manner, the problem of constitution evolves from a purely descriptive endeavor into an explanatory phenomenological investigation of the genesis or historicity and the facticity (Steinbock, 1998, p. 133) of the natural standpoint (i.e., Erfahrung). In this connection, we must keep in mind that the lifeworld is not solely a private affair of the ego, and Luft (2004a) therefore argued that the natural standpoint is informed by others, "the ones before me and after me, the ones I have never encountered and never will encounter" (p. 97). Thus, the gap that Husserl saw between his own and Heidegger's phenomenology narrows considerably with the emergence of genetic phenomenology due to its focus on the historicity of the natural attitude.

7   Epoché and Reduction
The Phenomenological Methods

Phenomenological research in the Husserlian tradition is usually classified as an inductive approach, which essentially conveys that we are in the business of building up a picture of the whole from bits of information. However, induction is not an adequate description of the phenomenological method (Edie, 2000, p. 58). Phenomenology is a comprehensive methodology guided by philosophical theories pertaining to the role consciousness plays in the constitution of our lifeworld, and to this end, the phenomenological analysis relies on the methods known as the epoché and reduction (Churchill, 2022, p. 9).

Some readers may have encountered the epoché for the first time when reading Moustakas (1994), who wholeheartedly embraces this concept and defined it in terms of bracketing the researcher's "prejudgements, biases and preconceived ideas of things" (p. 85). However, Moustakas misconstrued the true purpose of the epoché, which is to put out of action the natural attitude. Moustakas's (1994) misconceptions set in motion a reproduction of misunderstandings in the secondary literature. For example, Creswell (2007) stated that in his discussion of phenomenology, he advanced "a psychological perspective based on Moustakas (1994)" (p. 10). Thus, Creswell (2007) repeated Moustakas's definition of the epoché (see p. 59) and proposed that it can be applied by beginning the research with a "personal statement" (p. 61) about what prior experiences may influence researchers' analysis. While this is not irrelevant, it has nothing to do with dismantling the schism between an exterior world and an interior mind. Creswell (2007) went on to repeat Moustakas's statement that transcendental therefore means that "everything is perceived freshly, as for the first time" (p. 60), which is obviously not what transcendental means. Consequently, novice researchers may think they are doing transcendental research by bracketing their biases, but as we shall see in the following, this is far from the case.

DOI: 10.4324/9781003270058-7

Although the epoché is a presupposition of the reduction (Fink, 1995, p. 41), the epoché and reduction are not as such two separate steps. In theory, the epoché is a moment of phenomenological reduction, but for systematic reasons, it is often presented as consecutive moves. The fundamental point of the epoché and reduction is to reorient our gaze from what is experienced to the constitutive act of experiencing itself. Thus Husserl (2001a) stated, "We are plainly concerned with a quite necessary generalization of the question as to the conditions of the possibility of experience" (p. 74) and argued that it is necessary to differentiate between the "pure phenomenon of the mental act" (Husserl, 1973a, p. 24) and the ordinary psychological experience.

In this connection, we find the notion of the lived experiences repeated ad nauseam in applied research. However, in many studies, "the lived experience" is little more than a catchphrase used to invoke phenomenological credibility, where no further attempt to clarify is made. Thus, without a theoretical definition of what the researcher means by experience, it is virtually impossible to make sense of the epoché and reduction, and the researcher will grabble around the data without a clear purpose. Therefore, the following section introduces three distinct interpretations of the act of experiencing its correlated concept of the world that may serve as a framework for understanding what phenomenological reduction takes aim at.

Erlebnis and Reality

When Husserl (1977) wrote about experiences, he had two concepts in mind that are difficult to translate into English: "*Erlebnis*" and "*Erfahrung*" (p. 47). Erlebnis is usually translated as lived experience, which means a prereflective flow impression (Husserl, 2017, p. 209). In fact, perception is such an unreflected lived experience (Husserl, 1977, p. 23).

Hence, perception does not mean a point of view, an opinion, or an attitude. Perception is simply an intentional act, which gives reality to cognition in a certain way (Husserl, 2017, p. 114). However, these are not the kind of experiences we are fully aware of (Husserl, 2017, p. 52), and Husserl (1977) therefore stated that "the thinker knows nothing of his lived experiences of thinking but only of the thoughts" that he is thinking (p. 14). Nevertheless, the mental act of perceptions is what shapes the possibility of thought, and it is this experience that Husserl with his transcendental project of pure phenomenology wants to become an object of study so that he can achieve the mental seeing (Husserl, 1973a, p. 24) of essence.

Erfahrung and the Natural World

Merleau-Ponty (Edie, 2000) explained that in everyday life, we all live in the natural attitude, which is "the conviction that we are part of the world and subject to its action on us" (p. 56). Therefore, in the natural standpoint, our experience is not unreflected Erlebnis but "natural pre-scientific experience" (Husserl, 1977, p. 40). Thus, Husserl articulated "the general thesis of the natural attitude" (Luft, 2004a), which "consists of viewing the world as nature existing independent of an experiencing agent" (p. 76). This is essentially a belief, but one that empirical psychology accepts as a natural state of affairs and consequently articulates its research problems from this standpoint.

Husserl referred to this form of experience as Erfahrung and posited that "natural knowledge begins with experiences (Erfahrung) and remains within it" (2017, p. 51) and that *Erfarhung* allows us to "live in the belief in objectivity" (p. 146), in other words, in the belief of an objective world that we describe and make sense of through concepts and terminologies. Consequently, phenomenological psychology develops into a discipline that aims at elucidating the ontological content of psychological and scientific concepts (Kockelmans & Jager, 1967, p. 185). Thus, Merleau-Ponty argued that phenomenology is engaged in studying the distance between experience and science (Edie, 2000, p. 29) and in *Logical Investigations* (1900–1901), Husserl (2001a) explained that the purpose of phenomenological analysis was to "bring the ideas of logic, the logical concepts and laws, to epistemological clarity" (p. 96).

Active and Passive Synthesis and the Lifeworld (Lebenswelt)

Toward the end of his life, Husserl refocused on the natural standpoint, and instead of utilizing it as a staging point before entering the transcendental realm, he sat out to elucidate the genesis of the natural experience (Erfahrung). Husserl concluded that experience should be understood as a becoming through active and passive synthesis. By active synthesis, Husserl meant "different types of judgements" (Welton, 2003, p. 280), and by naming his last major work *Experience and Judgement* (*Erfahrung und Urteil*), Husserl indicated that he had come to see judging as the "fundamental objectifying act" (Drummond, 2003, p. 83).

While judging is an act, its content is made of a passive synthesis of ideal content, which can be understood as complexes of apperceived experiences that over time have sedimented into the individual's horizon. Welton (2003) referred to this as a level or "originary sensibility" "without active construction or interpretation" (p. 280). Thus, Barber (2015) posited that "something known creates an apperceptive type available for the experience of analogous objects" (p. 29), and therefore "we do not just experience individual objects but grasp them through types" (p. 29). Consequently, Luft (2004a) argued that the lifeworld is essentially "doxic" (p. 91) in the sense that the subject experience the world as a "truth-claim" (Vogt, 2012, p. 83).

For example, Welton (2003) explained that speech is an active synthesis, where we assign meanings to things and situations, but that these speech-acts take place "against a passive context of acquired language and prior established meanings fixed by a community of speakers" (p. 281). Thus, Husserl believed that all truth-claims indicated "earlier types of speech and then experiences" (p. 280) of the individual or the community from which they arise. Consequently, judgments "refer back to nested or implied meanings" and "to a context not directly expressed in their content" (p. 280).

Systematic Considerations

Having conceptualized what we mean by experience and world, we now have a clearer theoretical definition of the objects of our research. It is, however, important to understand that it is not so that people have either this or that type of experience. Experiencing is an all-inclusive phenomenon. Nevertheless, the researcher can still focus on certain aspects of experiencing relevant to a particular constitutive problem. However, this requires some mastery of the essential phenomenological techniques, and in the following, I will consider how the epoché and reduction may line up with the various conceptualization of experiencing.

For the sake of a systematic presentation two additional steps beyond the (a) epoché and (b) reduction, will be introduced: (c) transcendental reflections and (d) statement of meaning essence. The third step is a suggestion for how the researcher, after having operated empirically, can reconnect with the transcendental field, while the fourth step pertains to the statement of meaning essence and how to report our findings.

The Transcendental Epoché (1)

To understand Husserl's epoché, we must first grasp the context in which it was first seriously articulated in *Ideas*. In this book, Husserl's aim was not to provide a blueprint for psychological research but to establish a scientific philosophy based on an analysis of noetic acts (Husserl, 1970, p. 77). Hence, the human being is essentially "a thing which doubts, understands (conceives), affirms, denies, wills, refuses, which also imagines and feels" (Descartes, p. 10, 1911), and therefore the phenomenological shaping of the world always leads back to the regional objectivities within these mental acts.

With this scientific philosophical project in mind, Husserl (2017, p. 111) stated that "the epoché here in question will not be confused with that which positivism demands" and "we are not concerned at present with removing the preconceptions which troubles the pure positivity (Saklichkeit) of research." Instead, Husserl's (2017) purpose was to place the natural standpoint, which is the presupposition that the life-world (Lebenswelt) is the actual world, in brackets (see p. 111). Fink (1995, p. 42) described this moment as escaping "our captivation by the world," while Scheler (2009, p. 28) referred to the epoché as "shedding the spell of the environment." Husserl (2017) also bracketed the methods and theories from natural science and stated,

> I *disconnect them* all, *I make absolutely no use of their standards, I do not appropriate a single one of the propositions that enter into their systems, even though their evidential value is perfect, I take none of them, no one of them serves me for a foundation* – so long, that is, as it is understood, in the way these sciences themselves understand it, as a truth concerning the realities of this world. *I may accept it only after I have placed it in the bracket.*
>
> (p. 111)

Finally, Husserl (1973a) claimed that because of the epoché, "*every intellectual process and indeed every mental process whatever*, while being enacted, *can be made the object of a pure 'seeing': and understanding and is something absolutely given in this 'seeing.'* It is given as something that is, that is here and now, and whose being cannot be sensibly doubted" (p. 24).

The Phenomenological Psychological Epoché (1.2)

However, there is more than one epoché, and phenomenological psychology calls for a less radical starting point because the purpose is merely to examine the role psychological subjectivity plays in constituting the lifeworld. Hence, when studying the psychological ego, we cannot bracket the world, nor can we bracket the body. Therefore, we need a different kind of epoché.

In *Crisis*, Husserl (1970) expressed the need to explain why his phenomenological project is not descriptive psychology, and to this end, he actually went on to explain the kind of epoché he envisioned the psychological researcher should apply. In this version of the epoché, the researcher is not engaged in introspective activities, but "establishes in himself the disinterested spectator and investigator of himself as well as of all others" (p. 239) In other words, within the epoché, the world of the researcher and the world of the subjects are transformed into phenomena (Fink, 1995, p. xl), which means that we are not interested in the actual world and how it affects the individual, but in the lifeworld of meanings (Lebenswelt).

The question remains how we can justify that the researcher in the epoché can assume the role of disinterested spectator of other people's phenomenal experiences. Here we must remember that it is only in the natural attitude that the social world presents itself in terms of autonomous individuals. Thus, the fallacy of the natural attitude is that we assume that there is the same delimitation between social researchers and their subjects as there is between the botanist and plants. There is a significant difference because in the latter example a human subject studies an object (i.e., a plant), but in the first example, a subject studies another subject.

Thus, Scheler (1954) posited that "the spiritual person, as such, is intrinsically incapable of being treated as an object" (p. 224), and it is therefore not self-evident "that a man can only think his own thoughts and feel his own feelings" because we can understand other subjects like ourselves "by virtue of participation (or reproduction) in thought, volition or feeling" (p. 224). Thus Scheler (1954) argued while it is true that the mental reality of the individual is private, it is a false analogy to conclude that mental phenomena are as well, and "if the mental were only given to one person at a time, it could never be communicated" (p. 257).

Scheler (1954) therefore concluded "that just as the same mental content can be present in a multiplicity of acts, so it can also be present to a number of different individuals" (p. 258).

Along those lines, Englander and Morley (2021) stated, "[T]he epoché opens us to see how the world is profusely intertwined with both the researchers and the research participant's experience of it, characterizing a radically non-dogmatic and open-minded perspective towards psychological research." Thus, by putting out of play the assumptions of metaphysical naturalism, the epoché allows the boundaries between the mental life of subjects to become just a theoretical position instead of a rule and thereby affords the researcher the opportunity to participate in the subject's phenomenal lifeworld. However, we still refrain from imposing our own theoretical explanations (Englander & Morley, 2021), and Merleau-Ponty suggested that we shall not attempt to determine what caused expressive emotions, and we will not infer any form of causalities but "simply ask what emotion means and toward what it is tending" (Edie, 2000, p. 61).

The Genetic Phenomenological "Vocational Epoché" (1.3)

The overarching purpose of the epoché is to put out of play whatever in the natural attitude obstructs the researcher's access to the phenomenon (Butler, 2016). However, genetic phenomenological analysis takes as its starting point the individual's lifeworld and remains within it (Luft, 2011, p. 249), and therefore we do not need assistance from the transcendental nor the psychological epoché. Thus Husserl (1977, p. 41) stated that "it is taken for granted that we are remaining in the natural attitude, and that means nothing else but that we accept experiential being just as it gives itself." In this manner, the epoché, considered in the context of genetic phenomenology, assumes the character of a "vocational epoché" (Husserl, 1970, p. 137) that allows the researcher a particular focus on the lifeworld as it unfolds for the individual and communities. In this connection, Husserl (1970) stated that the researcher must consider the subject's lifeworld "a purely internal relating of the persons to things of which they are conscious, which are intentionally valid for them, within the world that is intentionally valid for them" (p. 238). Nevertheless, the researcher must abstain from participating in these validities (Churchill, 2022, p. 6).

What we could call the lifeworld epoché distinguishes itself from the phenomenological psychological epoché in the sense that we are not discerning whether the individuals' lifeworld correlates with their direct experiences or whether they are apperceiving experiences of other individuals. Thus Scheler (1954) argued,

> [I]t may also happen that the thought of another is not presented as such, but as a though or ours. Such is the case, for instance, in "unconscious reminiscence" of things read or communicated. It also occurs when, imbued with a genuine tradition, we accept the thoughts of others, e.g. of our parents or teachers, as thoughts of our own.
>
> (p. 245)

Hence, within the natural attitude, we are simply not able to predetermine the criteria of the content that "populates" our apperceptive glance.

The Transcendental Reduction (2)

Giorgi (2010) argued that "no claim for phenomenological status can be made if some legitimate type of reduction is not used" (p. 18). Further, Luft (2011) argued that to reject the reduction is to reject the fundamental phenomenological axiom that consciousness constitutes our world as a meant-world and stated, "All achievements of phenomenology either explicitly or tacitly take place in the space opened up by the reduction" (p. 252). Thus, the term "reduction" simply means a leading back to the realm of transcendental subjectivity that constitutes reality.

Husserl's elaboration of the reduction was in the service of establishing a scientific philosophy of transcendental phenomenology. He believed that the fact that we all roughly experience the same reality indicates that our experiences are contingent on a transcendental subjectivity that objectifies the world in a certain way, which in the final analysis means that transcendental subjectivity is transcendental intersubjectivity. Thus, by enacting phenomenological reduction, he suggested it would be possible to mentally see these regional objectivities of intentionality, which he referred to as essence. In other words, if thoughts were fish and the river was thinking, Husserl's transcendental reduction would empty the river of fish and then study the stream of water to understand how the essential nature of this stream correlates with the kind of fish that can appear in the river.

To facilitate the "apprehension of essence," Husserl introduced a technique referred to under many labels such as "eidetic variation," "eidetic reduction" "free variation," or "imaginative variation." Eidetic variation is to phenomenological research what hypotheses testing is to deductive research. Thus, Husserl (2017, p. 199) stated that "in phenomenology as in all eidetic sciences, free fancies, assume a privileged position over against perceptions" (p. 199) In other words, when enacting the reduction apodictic, knowledge takes precedence over empirical knowledge.

The technique consists of conceiving the perceived object or situation as a possibility among many other varying possibilities to determine the invariant aspects of the phenomenon. Whatever remains the same regarding the experience, no matter how we conceive of it, is to be considered apodictic truths in contrast to the empirical truths derived from observations (Belt, 2021). Where apodictic truths are universal because they are derived from transcendental subjectivity, empirical truths are far less reliable because they are derived from often incomplete observations of merely a case. For example, the perception of a cube can be accomplished from multiple angles, each of which represents the object in a different way, but never in its entirety; however, the eidetic analysis of variation demonstrates that it is essential for a cube to have six sides of equal sizes and, if it does not, then it is no longer a cube. In a similar fashion, we can turn the eidetic analysis toward the act of perception itself. In this manner, we can grasp the regional objectivity of perception or its essence from the fact that irrespective of the angle of perception, what remained invariant was a three-dimensional perspective. Thus, the apodictic truth about the act of visual perception is perspective.

As social research is essentially empirical, we can have nothing more than a theoretical interest in transcendental reduction because, from the natural standpoint, the researcher is unable to apprehend the distinction between thoughts and thinking in other people. However, Husserl (1970) argued that psychological researchers may from the perspective of the epoché execute the transcendental move to further enrich their understanding of how their subjects' lifeworld is constituted and stated,

> [A]ll the new sorts of apperceptions which are exclusively tied to the phenomenological reduction, together with the new sort of language – all this, which before was complete hidden and inexpressible, now flows into self-objectification, into my psychic life and becomes apperceived as its newly revealed intentional background of constitutive accomplishments.
>
> (p. 210)

However, Merleau-Ponty's study of embodiment revealed that certain forms of intentionality are observable. Thus, Scheler (1954, p. 10) argued that we can have insight into others "insofar as we treat their bodies as a field of expression for their experiences" and from this follows that we are not only talking about an insight into the subject's inner life but to "all that goes along with it" including the environment (p. 218). In this connection, Sousa (2014, p. 46) argued that the phenomenological analysis could include emotional gestures. In this manner, signifying body language is likely the closest we will get to observing intentionality outside our own introspective endeavors. Nevertheless, it is difficult although not impossible to conceive of a phenomenological study that is based purely on body language observation.

The Phenomenological Psychological Reduction (2.1)

The purpose of the phenomenological psychological reduction is to provide a tentative answer to the question of how subjectivity contributes toward the constitution of the type of situations and species of objects people encounter (Spiegelberg, 1971, p. 693). Husserl (1977) readily talked about the phenomenological reduction in the context of descriptive psychology (p. 153), but only in his final years did he begin to elaborate on a distinct "[p]henomenological-psychological reduction" (Husserl, 1970, p. 244). However, his thoughts on this matter came across as having the purpose of demonstrating why his transcendental reduction was not psychological. For example, Husserl (1970) explained,

> [W]hether the perceived [object] exists or not, whether the perceiving person is mistaken about this or not, and also whether I, the psychologist, who in my empathetic understanding of the person unhesitantly concur in the belief in the perceived [object], am mistaken about it or not – this must remain irrelevant for me as a psychologist. None of this may enter into the psychological description of the perception.
>
> (p. 236)

From the quote, we can see that there is not a very clear distinction between the phenomenological psychological epoché and the reduction, which is not surprising since these moves are two sides of the same coin. The fact is that a systematic development of phenomenological psychology was left to Husserl's followers to complete. The point of departure is the admission, echoed by Heisenberger and Schrödinger in Chapter 5, that natural science never came to a real understanding of the involvement of the subjective in the objectification of nature.

Kockelmans and Jager (1967) explained that in the natural attitude, the world is "given in an immediate, prescientific experience as the world of our actual life" (p. 146), which is what Husserl referred to as Erfahrung. They further argued that if the world was not first given in natural experience, there would be "no basis on which any science could form" (p. 146). It is therefore the purpose of the phenomenological psychological reduction to "turn away from the cultural world" (p. 148) and return to this immediate experience. Kockelmans and Jager (1967) defined this immediate experience as a "structural unity of reality" (p. 150), where things and situations are apperceived in a manner that includes all the surplus data from our experience horizon. They ultimately conceptualized it as a "gestalt" (p. 154) that links space and time with the immediate experience. Steinbock (1995) is therefore correct when he suggested that the psychological reduction opens up "the structure of subjectivity itself, disclosing the horizons of intentional life" (p. 56).

To this end, the researchers will attempt to elucidate "the original relationship between I and the world, between the ego and any worldly structure whatsoever" (Kockelmans & Jager, 1967, p. 317) by deploying the method of eidetic variation and in this way apprehend the "variety of shapes conscious experience can assume" (Bower, 2020, p. 187). This may sound a bit poetic, but in applied terms, the purpose of the psychological reduction is to elucidate in what ways the gestalt of the subject's natural experiences corresponds with the conceptual reality of science as well as the delimitations of scientific domains (Kockelmans & Jager, 1967). For example, all scientific psychological concepts are ultimately derived from natural experience, and because they are used by psychologists to objectify the lived experiences of subjects, it is tremendously important that they are not far off the mark.

Thus, Giorgi's modified Husserlian reduction begins with narrowing the researcher's frame of reference to the field of psychology (Englander & Morley, 2021). While the researcher focuses on immediate and ideally naive experiences from everyday situations, this form of psychological reduction allows the researcher to articulate a meaning essence that is relevant to the "discipline of psychology" (Englander & Morley, 2021). Giorgi (2009) explained that in a certain sense, what has to be expressed is constituted by the phenomenological psychological attitude of the researcher. Because the psychological dimension "is not just lying there fully blown, ready to be picked out. It has to be detected, drawn out and elaborated" (p. 131). In this manner, Giorgi (1985) shifted the constitutional problem from the intentionality of the first-person point of view to the intentionality of the researcher as the question of constitution is transported from the subjects' lifeworld into a construed "psychological reality" "that has to be constituted by the psychologist" (p. 11).

There is nothing peculiar about this move because this is exactly what a professional therapist does when engaging a client. However, our research subjects are not patients, and this shift does beckon the question, who is the real subject? The participants or the researcher? The answer is likely both, as the outcome of Giorgi's reduction appears to be co-constituted. For example, Englander and Morley (2021) elaborated on the procedure of eidetic or "imaginative variation," but their actual application consists of the researchers varying their subjects' phenomenal experiences in their own imagination. Moustakas (1994) proposed the same technique, but the validity of eidetically varying other people's experiences is somewhat dubious because it is almost impossible to ascertain whether the insights we arrive at originated from the eidetic process or from the preexisting theoretical knowledge that trained psychologists have.

This problem is somewhat mitigated by working with more than one subject, as this method brings the variation out of the researcher's head and into the sampling procedure. Belt (2021) referred to this as sampling "real-life-deviations" accomplished through "detailed person level descriptions." In this connection, Husserl (1970) emphasized that the reduction must be performed "in such a way that it is exercised individually to "painstakingly extract for oneself the meaning of these subjects" (p. 247) because the psychological subjectivity of each subject is always a separate reality.

Genetic Phenomenology and the Ontological Reduction (2.2)

The genetic phenomenological reduction aims at deconstructing the natural experience (Erfahrung) to uncover the structures of the original lifeworld of doxic experiences, which is the individual's "belief-of-being." Hence, Husserl sought an "Abbau" or unbuilding of the natural standpoint into its "formative elements" (Alves, 2021, p. 209). This reflective procedure can therefore best be described as an ontological reduction.

The reduction is regressive as it entails a "questioning back" (Steinbock, 1995, p. 82) (*Rückfragen*) from the actual world experience to the operations of subjectivity (Husserl, 1973b, p. 50), where the researchers will attend to the presuppositions that serve as the "constitutive condition of world-experience" (Steinbock, 1995, p. 84). Thus, Husserl (1973b, p. 353) explained that when people refer to the facts of a situation, they simply engage in the business of applicating aprioric truth-claims. Hence, Husserl (1973b) stated that the task of the reduction is the seeing of ideas (p. 349), which in the context of the genetic analysis can be considered what people hold as "a prori truths" that "precede all factuality" (p. 353) of their lifeworld experience.

In this connection, Husserl (1973b) argued, "[E]very conceivable attempt to exhibit the sources of justification which confer a rational privilege on any such judgments, as opposed to their contraries, comes to nothing" (p. 392) and that

> the only thing one can do here is to explore the psychological origin of the relevant judgments and concept, i.e., search out, in the actual human psyche the source from which arises the semblance of rationality of these judgements and, above all, also to explain genetically

how in general we come to believe, beyond what is given in perception and memory, in what is to come, how *the feeling of necessity* arises, and how it is confused with that objective necessity.

(p. 392)

Further, Husserl (1973b) argued that we are dealing with "an active believing cognizance of which we are aware" (p. 62) and which is, therefore, "freely available, preservable and communicable" (p. 61). Hence, genetic phenomenology aligns well with applied research because the data is accessible.

In this connection, Eidelson and Eidelson (2003) found that "individual-level core beliefs" (p. 188) primarily come into view from narratives about interpersonal relationships, for example, situations playing out with friends, family members, colleagues, and more importantly from encounters with the otherness of strangers. Hence, a regressive phenomenological analysis of natural experience could potentially assist in elucidating theories pertaining to prejudice and bias. However, such regressive analysis could also take place at the group level, where Eidelson and Eidelson (2003) suggested studying "collective narratives based on broader cultural understandings of in-group–out-group relationships" (p. 203). In this connection, Husserl (1970), in Appendix III to *The Crisis of European Sciences and Transcendental Phenomenology*, explained how researchers could proceed with studies of

factual persons, peoples and [historical] times, and the things supposed by them to exist in their supposed worlds, which appear to them concretely, intuitively, in such and such a way, which are apperceived as such mythologically or in some other way, the natures experienced by them, the cultures which existed for them and motivate them.

(p. 320)

Husserl referred to these themes as "leading clues" and "ideal possibilities" (as cited in Steinbock, 1998, p. 141) that may serve as starting points for working out of a lifeworld (Lebenswelt) ontology, where the researcher will attempt to explain what an experience means to the subjects by describing the "constitutive contributions" (Lohmar, 2014, p. 267) of previous experiences which are now sedimented as memory-beliefs (Ofengenden, 2014).

In this manner, we are interpreting "the experiential history" (Lohmar, 2014, p. 266) in the light of time, and Steinbock (1995) therefore argued that temporality must serve as a systematic theme for our interpretation of the genesis of natural experience (Erfahrung; Steinbock, 1995, p. 49).

In this manner, we begin to see a convergence between Husserl's epistemology and Heidegger's analysis of Dasein as the researcher's interpretative horizon becomes time. The main difference between the two thinkers would be Husserl's insistence that a genetic phenomenological analysis of the lifeworld is just another starting point that ultimately leads to insight into a world constituted through transcendental subjectivity (Luft, 2004b. p. 250)

Reflections on Phenomenologizing (3)

Merleau-Ponty (1978) criticized natural science for tending to "force the phenomenal universe into categories, which makes sense only in the universe of science" (p. 11), but despite our self-proclaimed virtues, we are doing exactly the same in applied phenomenology because we are shaping the research outcomes by our presumption of intentionality. In this connection, Fink (1995) argued that the "phenomenologizing onlooker" (p. 99) tends to be self-referential when thematizing the experiences of others. For example, Wertz (1985) explained that the meaning-units in the phenomenological psychological analysis are "meaning-units-for-the-researcher" (p. 165). In this manner, the researchers inadvertently become a theme within the thematization because it is their "existential baseline" that is the reference point of the analysis and not the subjects'.

Hence, we must place our "own inquiry in question" (Fink, 1995, p. 37) and reflect on how we came to judge our subjects' disclosures to be phenomenologically revelatory and ask, "How am I understanding the phenomenon such that this statement reveals it?" or "What does this statement reveal about the phenomenon? How is it relevant?" (Wertz, 1985, p. 175). Thus, Fink (1995) argued while "constitutive analyses result in truths about constituting" (p. 50), these are not truths in themselves, because in the epoché and reduction, "we annul precisely the natural concept of experience" (p. 51). Therefore, our findings are theoretical truths for phenomenologizing. In other words, the researchers have theoretical experience as they apperceive others from a distinct theoretical horizon of phenomenology, and our descriptive language is infused with all of the presuppositions of this frame of reference and more so from our professional fields of practice. Hence, the researcher is "enworlded" (p. 99), and in this connection, Fink (1995) saw a risk that our terminologies and analogies may "lord it over the 'transcendental' sense; overrun and conceal it" (p. 92).

Specifically, the risk is that the researcher psychologizes the experience by positing a cause-and-effect relationship between the external world and intentionality and in this manner forgets that we are dealing with a world as intended and not with an actual world. Likewise, we must not make the mistake to assume that intentionality causes phenomenal experiences. In fact, Fink (1995) argued that "subjectivity is not something that first is and then constitutes, but that it is in the constitutive process in which the world comes about that it constitutes itself" (p. 97). However, Fink acknowledged that this is less of a risk in "smaller concrete constitutive analyses" (p. 97). In other words, the further the reduction moves toward the transcendental realm, the more problematic our status as enworlded becomes (p. 13).

However, Husserl (2017) stated that "the bracketing of thesis should not hinder our description; we just refrain from setting into action said thesis" (p. 265). This means that Husserl's disinterested spectator now must become a disinvested communicator by acknowledging that the professional nomenclature that might be used when articulating the research findings must be considered as just euphemisms and analogies. Thus, Fink (1995) argued that the researcher "makes language into a mere means for the explication for which he himself has at his disposal no suitable language of his own" (p. 94). This means that the researcher should consider the distance of their language from the language of their subjects'.

Wertz (1985) therefore stated that the "researcher must constantly return to the original description given by the subject in order to verify, modify, or negate his reflective understanding" (p. 177). In this connection, the secondary literature on qualitative research typically suggests that member-check or in-group verification is the way to bridge the gap between the subjects' and the researchers' experiences. However, within the applied phenomenological psychological literature, we find a clear rejection (Giorgi, 2009) of this form of triangulation. The argument is that the phenomenological psychological researcher has a theoretical experience within the reduction in contrast to our subjects' reflections, which are taking place in the natural attitude. Thus, the research subjects are not in a position to validate our findings. While this position may make analytical sense, its proponents overlook the fact that (a) we are not articulating the findings in the reduction but in the natural attitude, (b) the researchers could explain their findings in layman's terms, and, finally, (c) validation is not verification but an attempt to bridge a gap between two perspectives on the same situation (i.e., the subjects' perspective from within the situation and the researchers' perspective from within their professional practices; Dreyfuss, 1995, p. 36).

In addition, we should reflect the status of our subjects as embodied, where we recognize that their bodies are fields of experiences and expressions and that gestures not only reflect their experiences but also turn around and signify them and their lifeworld. Thus, in our analysis, we must be careful not to give priority to the spoken word over the gesture, which can be challenging for a researcher who relies only on interview transcripts. By omitting observational data from the interview situation, we are not only depriving ourselves of a valuable source of data, but we are also giving priority to the more articulate of our subjects and therefore inadvertently perpetuating marginalization.

Statement of Meaning Essence (4)

After having completed the various types of reductions, helped along by eidetic variation and reflection on our phenomenologizing, we must try to make a statement about our findings, which is often referred to as the essence. However, essence is really an outcome that only pertains to transcendental phenomenology, where the philosophizers achieve mental seeing of the regional objectification within intentional acts. As we have discovered in the previous chapters, this is not a level of elucidation that we can achieve in phenomenological psychology.

Hence, James viewed the "essence" as the sum of the most important features of an experience (Wilshire, 1969), and Merleau-Ponty claimed,

> [A]n essence is a meaning inherent in a particular set of experiences. It has *some* claim to universality insofar as it is the essence of a particular phenomenon, so future experiences of that item (future instances of that phenomenon) will unfold in accordance to that form.
>
> (As cited in Romdenh-Romluc, 2018, p. 354)

In other words, we are reporting on the "gestalt" of the experience (i.e., those structures that are necessary for an experience to be a certain type of experience and not another). As we have seen in the previous sections, the purpose is to confront the temporality of natural experience with the static concepts of science.

In this connection, phenomenological psychology has played an important role in developing a detailed understanding of the experience of mental illness and contributed to the clarification of the diagnostic nomenclature of psychology and psychiatry (Kendler & Parnas, 2008. p. 6). Thus, the researcher may report findings from a phenomenological psychological study in terms of the structures of an experience that are essential for the meaning of concepts used within the field of psychology or within other fields where psychological concepts are applied – for example, education and organizational leadership. Consequently, such reporting is entirely descriptive, where the researcher in general and somewhat abstract terms tries to convey the extended structures pertaining to the whatness and aboutness of an experience, while at the same time redeeming these inferences in the data. Englander and Morley (2021) referred to this as "zooming-in on the unique and minute details" while at the same time "zooming out" to see the big picture and contexts.

The task of reporting is somewhat different in a genetic phenomenological study as we try to illuminate what is true about the experience based on the phenomenological assumption that the individual's horizon of experience is "always limited by horizons that have been previously constituted" (Sousa, 2014, p. 30). In other words, we are zooming in on the fundamental beliefs that our subjects hold and how they are deployed in judging what things are. For example, Eidelson and Eidelson (2003) stated, "[M]any of these organizing beliefs about the self, the environment, and the future are formed relatively early in life and serve a useful purpose," but "there is considerable evidence that habitual modes of perceiving and thinking can pose problems as well" (p. 182).

In this connection, Sousa (2014, p. 38) explained how "traumatic experience causes the temporal awareness of the past to congeal in the present, so that one remains captive there or returns constantly to it." Therefore, a statement of meaning essence from the perspective of a genetic phenomenological analysis could pertain to maladaptation resulting from a conflict between sedimented trauma that the situation we investigate has stimulated to actualize as "truth-claims" (Vogt, 2012, p. 83), which appear abnormal considering the "face value" of the situation in itself. The terms abnormal and normal are here to be understood in a philosophical context, where normal simply means that the truth-claims about a situation reasonably coincide with the actualities of the situation (Steinbock, 1995, p. 130).

Eidelson and Eidelson (2003) found that this is not only true at the individual level but also at the group level and posited that "collective core beliefs or group worldviews are the templates through which groups and group members interpret their shared experience" (p. 183). In this connection, their research identified five maladaptive belief domains appearing individually as well as collectively and tend to be associated with intergroup conflicts: "Superiority, injustice, vulnerability, distrust, and helplessness" (p. 183). In this connection, Rozbicki (2015) argued that culture is "what people believe they are and what they live for" (p. 8), and although these beliefs are subjective, "they are experienced as natural reality. This reality, constituted and co-constructed in the process of communication, should concern us as the subject of our study and not the question whether it is a reflection of scientifically understood objective reality" (p. 8).

Examples of Phenomenological Psychology

Wertz (1985) attempted to illuminate what criminal victimization is through a psychological phenomenological investigation of 50 survivors, who each had different experiences hereunder, "assaults, robbery, burglary, theft, attempted rape" (p. 161). In this way, Wertz zoomed in on the experience of one subject who survived an attempted rape and reported his findings in accordance with Giorgi's method.

The first stage was the pure interview transcript, where the woman's account of the experience was somewhat temporally unstructured and also contained elements that might not be directly relevant to the experience of victimization. Therefore, the next stage was to reconfigure the interview into meaning-units. This move was part of a phenomenological psychological reduction, where the researcher attempted to identify the constituents of this experience and subsequently placed these in a temporal order that matched the pattern of the actual event. In this manner, Wertz (1985) explained that "the researcher's comprehension is challenged to find relevance anyway it can, and his choices are based in his specific ability to do so" (p. 167). We are thus reminded of the vocational nature of Giorgi's reduction, where the phenomenological psychologist does not bracket his professional knowledge about victimization but rather applies it to understand the psychology of victimization.

Thus, Wertz (1985) concluded that three elements were the constituents of the victimization experience: "an other's detrimentality – a potential rapist"; the subject's "own vulnerability, impotence and loss of agency"; and "the absence of helpful community" (p. 180). In turn, victimization integrated as a constitutive component of the subject's experience horizon, where "expectation and avoidance of victimization" became part of the subject's "daily interpersonal relations" (p. 187).

Subsequently, the researcher must determine from a range of different victimization experiences the invariant structures of victimization.

This is not achieved simply by comparing cases and language, but through eidetic variation, where the researcher applied his own imagination to examine "any and all possible variations of being criminally victimized to see what is invariably necessary for a phenomenon to qualify as an instance of it" (Wertz, 1985, p. 190). Consequently, Wertz (1985) came to the conclusion that

> being criminally victimized is a disruption of daily routine and a shattering of its taken for granted horizon of social harmony which compels one, despite his resistance, to face his fellow as predator and himself as prey, isolated from any helpful community.
>
> (p. 192)

From this follows that "the victim is pervasively attuned to being victimized and begins to live the meanings of victimization throughout many facts of his world" (p.192).

Paley (2017, p. 45) questioned how phenomenological psychologists manage to identify the phenomenon and how they know that the interview data describes said phenomenon. Paley's (2017) concerns are based on a misconception of phenomena because when Wertz (1985) talks about the phenomenon of victimization, he is not referring to phenomenon in the phenomenological sense. As the previous chapters have clarified, phenomena are either ontic or ontological, and criminal victimization is therefore not a phenomenon; it is a concept or what we can call an ideal object.

In this connection, Schutz (1972, p. 190) demonstrated that positing a concept as a "free entity," and placing this in the position of the phenomenon effectively reverses the reduction because the researcher de facto jettisons the subject's constitutive role from the analysis. Thus, confounding the phenomenon with an ideal object (concept) inserts an element of extant theoretical bias as well as deduction in the analyses because the procedures inadvertently organize around connecting the data to the concept. However, this does not run counter to the phenomenological psychological research program, which according to Kockelmans and Jager's (1967) definition appears to be somewhat abductive as the gestalt of the natural experience confronts psychological concepts. Hence, Wertz (1985) is in fact engaging in an ontological clarification of psychological concepts, which is entirely legitimate because this is indeed the problem that Husserl and the Dutch School conceived phenomenological psychology should engage with.

The problem lies elsewhere (i.e., in the skills and ability of the researcher). Hence, the modified phenomenological psychological reduction risks falling prey to what Giorgi (2009) referred to as an "eclectic theoretical attitude" of the therapist "who recognize common psychological characteristics or pathologies prior to any theoretical interpretation" (p. 183), which is another word for the situation in which the researchers find what they were looking for in the data. Thus Husserl (2017) warned,

> [A]nalogies, which press upon us may, prior to real intuition, supply us with conjectures as to the essential relations of things, and from these may be drawn inferences that lead us farther forward; but in the end the conjectures must be redeemed by the real vision of essential connexions. So long as this is not done we have no result that we can call phenomenological.
>
> (p. 210)

Example of Genetic Phenomenology

The long-term problem with traumatic victimization is that it short-circuits the plasticity of memories around one or more past events in a way that continuously skewers our beliefs about new situations and their possibilities. This in turn may lead to ongoing maladaptive behaviors that sediment in our horizon. In other words, instead of conceiving trauma as an event with a defined beginning and end that causes a specific psychological state and associated behaviors, the genetic phenomenological researcher must conceive of victimization as a temporal phenomenon. Consequently, genetic phenomenology focuses on how sedimented apperceptions and maladaptive behaviors play a role in building a victimization lifeworld characterized by enduring "existential tension and conflicts" (Sousa, 2017, p. 98).

Wilde (2022) argued that mental health problems in the aftermath of violent experiences are not sufficiently explained by phenomenological causality. Thus, Wilde's (2022) research demonstrated that the experience of childhood rape alters the individual's passive and active syntheses. While the concrete experience may recede from the victim's thematic focus it still "assumes a place within the non-thematized horizon" (Barber, 2015, p. 29) that in turn will inform how others will be judged as basically untrustworthy throughout the victim's life. Trust in others has simply been replaced with distrust from what Welton (2003) referred to as the "secondary sensibility" (p. 280) of passive synthesis. Consequently, the trauma of rape changes the ideal content of the victim's active synthesis of judging others, which becomes the genesis of additional traumatic experiences when encountering other people. Thus, Wilde (2022) argued that it is only when instances of the victim's inability to trust others and what follows from this, begin to accumulate that the full extent of the trauma can be understood.

In contrast, DeRobertis and Bland (2020) studied 11 subjects' accounts of cross-cultural encounters and submitted their disclosures about overcoming the sense of threat stoked by the outgroup's otherness to a genetic phenomenological analysis. The applied method was aligned with Giorgi (2009) and similar to those applied by Wertz (1985). The researchers found that when the subjects actively engage the others, they began to apperceive their cultural differences from the perspective of sameness as these "others" were perceived to share the same kind of struggles and sufferings as the subjects themselves.

Thus, DeRobertis and Bland (2020) demonstrated that the accumulation of cross-cultural encounters sedimented new meanings that gradually changed the base assumption of danger to trust. In other words, the constitutive presuppositions of the subjects' judging-acts were modified as new apperceptions over time sedimented into their horizons and made a new apperceptive type available for the experience of the others. The outcome of this study indicated that cohabitation is a possibility that can be actualized when individuals are open to learning from their encounters. The challenge with DeRobertis and Bland (2020) is that they largely skip demonstrating their reflexive procedures, which makes it difficult to critically evaluate their findings. Thus, researchers need to strike a balance between economic writing and trustworthiness. In this case, a more detailed explanation of the reflective steps would have enhanced trustworthiness.

In contrast, an ethnographic study of Western expatriates' attitudes toward Chinese people in Shanghai (Larsen & Wolowitz, 2015) demonstrated how a regressive analysis can be accomplished in communities. Two online communities were chosen with a combined membership of around 100,000 unique users that produced over 800,000 online posts. The first step of the analysis consisted of sampling 113 dense discussion threads. Thereafter the researchers proceeded to quantify the attitude tendency, and to this end, Eagly and Chaiken's (1993) earlier-mentioned tripartite conceptual model was applied. The results were that "78% of the evaluative statements" (p. 185) from sampled threads were negative and because the framework equates tendency with attitude, the researchers concluded that the attitude was overwhelmingly negative. Subsequently, the researchers engaged in a deconstruction (Abbau) of this quantified objectification of expatriate attitude into its constitutive elements of core beliefs.

The outcome demonstrated that superiority beliefs (p. 193) were a pervasive theme in the community members' judgments of the local population and type of language, and the metaphors used reflected documented prejudice stretching back to the 19th century. Thus, a thematic description of the prejudiced content was presented as a tentative ontological clarification of the attitude. In addition, the outcome of this study indicated that historic superiority beliefs were readily assumed as a "group norm" (p. 194) and that new members were socialized into these beliefs and consequently that these beliefs were not exclusively a question of apperception of own perceptions, but that the apperceptions of community members' disclosures appeared just as salient for the genesis of the documented attitude.

8   Existential Phenomenology

The schism within phenomenology can be boiled down to a question of what has priority in the analysis: essence or existence. In this way, Heidegger came to see the notions of a hidden transcendental subjectivity, an inner ego, psychological subjectivity, et cetera, as constructs that trap us in an almost religious worldview where something must beget something. It seems we need the idea of subjectivity to explain why we think what we do and the notion of the ego to explain our desires and ambitions, and in this way, the human being becomes a layered construct with a degree of separation from the world we inhabit. Thus, Heidegger (Guignon, 1983, p. 13) chides Descartes for originating a worldview, which essentially requires the philosopher "to prove the reality of the outer world."

Heidegger's phenomenology is therefore quite different from Husserl's in the sense that an experience is not the operation of "a cognitive faculty interior to the subject" (Heidegger, 1988, p. 66). Instead, an experience is what the human being cares about. Therefore, we must not confuse caring with subjectivity; instead, we must conceive caring in terms of engaging with things and being with other people. Consequently, the experience is a worldly event understood as an "experience with." Thus, Heidegger (1988, p. 289) argued that "we understand ourselves by way of things," and Dasein, therefore, "comes toward itself from out of the things" (p. 289). This led Boss (1982, p. 41) to conclude that "as things cannot be without man, man cannot exist as he is without that which he encounters."

In other words, the experience is an interpretation of the relationship between Dasein and something other than Dasein. Thus Boss (1982) argued that "the human being and what appears in the light of human existence are mutually dependent on each other" (p. 42), and consequently, the existential relationship between Dasein and the world, "supports everything, insofar as it brings forth both the

DOI: 10.4324/9781003270058-8

appearance of things and man's Dasein" (p. 42). Thus, the thesis is that the phenomenon of the human being Dasein exists in a behavioral mode of being-with-the-world, which existentially determines Dasein's own Being as well as all other Being of what we encounter (Heidegger, 2010, p. 117). Heidegger (2010, p. 116) therefore argued that "the world of Dasein is a with-world (Mitwelt)" and not the constituted Lebenswelt we find in Husserl's phenomenology.

Heidegger is however not alone in defining existential phenomenology. On the contrary, it is a range of phenomenological approaches that share the conviction that elucidating the Being of beings requires an interpretation of the Being of the human being (Koloskov, 2022). It can be argued that Heidegger's phenomenology has an ontological character, as he is committed to phenomenology as a method for the elucidation of what Being is (Boss, 1982, p. 45). However, the conceptualization of Dasein, as essentially world disclosure (Boss, 1982, p. 43), inspired thinkers such as Jean-Paul Sartre and Paul Ricoeur to consider not only the ontological question pertaining to the *whatness* of Being but also the anthropological question of how beings are and how that discloses Being as a value proposition as well as a character. The following presentation will therefore consider the ideas of the patriarchs of existential phenomenology, Heidegger, Sartre, and Ricoeur, who each in their own way attempted to outline approaches to the study of Being from an interpretation of the what, the how, and the who of Dasein's Being with the world.

The Research Domain of Ontological Phenomenology

Heidegger first came to phenomenology as one of Husserl's students and prominent followers, but in fact, Heidegger ended up rejecting Husserl's theory of constitution because it almost requires the researcher to prove that the world is actually real. Thus, Heidegger (2010), in his seminal work *Being and Time*, concluded that transcendental phenomenology has a problem with explaining how an essence confined to an "inner sphere" of a "knowing subject comes out of its inner sphere, into one that is other and external" (p. 60).

Heidegger claimed that the question of Being and the meaning of being had been overlooked by Husserl and therefore made Being the arch of his scholarly life. When Heidegger talked about Being, he did not mean actual physical beings. Instead, he was referring to the phenomenon that emerges when Dasein comports itself to the world (Heidegger, 1988, p. 16). Thus, Heidegger (1988) stated that Being is what we think about our world when we say, "[T]his is such and such, that other is not so" (p. 14). Thus, understanding what things are in their respective categories is essential for empirical science, and Heidegger's point is that the phenomenon of the human being he calls Dasein is indispensable for the constitution of what things are since the world science is preoccupied with is the world for human beings.

In other words, Dasein is the ontico-ontological foundation of all Being. Thus, when Dasein cares about certain things, it transforms from a state of "being there" to a state "being with" (Mitdasein). Thus, Marder (2011) argued that the preposition "with" in "being with" is how Dasein draws together "the ontic and the ontological, the existential and the categorical." Therefore, the notion of having an experience with something is at the same time positing of that something. In this manner, the being of that something is an interpretation of the belonging together of what appears ontically true about an object or situation and the ontological truths Dasein already knows. By conceptualizing Dasein as an ontico-ontological unity and Mitdasein as constitutive of what things are, Heidegger resolved the problem that still haunts Husserl's epistemological approach, which is that noetic knowledge can never exist without its intended object. In an applied context, this means that for the researcher, there can never be an empirical distinction between appearances and appearing, which makes it difficult to apprehend the phenomenological shaping.

While we now understand the ontological difference between beings and Being, the meaning of Being is still out of reach. In this connection, Heidegger argued that Being must be understood in light of time because Dasein's existential comportment is always temporal, as it cares about things in order to and for the sake of something and is therefore always leaning into the future while at the same time understanding its possibilities to be from the past. Thus, Heidegger (2010) argued that a person's entire ontology is anchored in temporality and that "time is the horizon of every understanding and interpretation of being" (p. 17). In other words, the meaning of Dasein's being is its temporality, and phenomenology must be conceived as "a method of ontology" (p. 20). Hence the Greek root "ontos" signifies Being and the "logos is time itself" (Marder, 2011).

The Research Methods of Ontological Phenomenology

Heidegger (1988) argued that "the phenomenon in the phenomenological understanding is always just what constitutes Being" and that "phenomenology is the science of the Being of beings" (p. 33). However, the phenomenon of the human being we call Dasein is unique in terms of its preoccupation with its own Being. Dasein is therefore openness to the world, and it is only by interrogating Dasein that Being of any kind can be disclosed (Rae, 2010).

Thus, Heidegger (2010) stated that the phenomenon

> is something that does *not* show itself initially and for the most part, something that is *concealed* [verbogen] in contrast to what initially and for the most part does show itself. But, at the same time, it is something that essentially belongs to what initially and for the most part shows itself, indeed in such a way that it constitutes its meaning and ground.
>
> (p. 33)

He was referring to Dasein. Therefore, phenomenology becomes a method for how we can "elucidate the existence of Dasein" (Heidegger, 1988, p. 154), and Heidegger (2010) thus stated that "phenomenology signifies primarily a concept of method" (p. 26) that has as its purpose to develop a fundamental ontology of Being.

In Heidegger's (1988) view, an analysis of Dasein must accomplish two goals: (a) "[o]ntologically distinguishing one being of a peculiar sort from other beings" and (b) "exhibiting the Being of that being" (p. 154). The key point is that due to Dasein's ability to comport, Heidegger makes Dasein the measure of the Being of all beings, including Dasein's own Being.

It is however difficult for Dasein to come face-to-face with Being and consequently also challenging for the researcher to accomplish this task. In this connection, Heidegger (1968, p. 110) reminded us that

> just as it is with bats' eyes in respect of daylight, so it is with our mental vision in respect of those things which are by nature most apparent (that is, the presence of all that is present). The Being of being is the most apparent; and yet, we normally do not see it – and if we do, only with difficulty.

The reason is that we tend to psychologize any analysis with a human subject, and we like to understand ourselves as having this inner person Freud called the ego and blame our failings on a subconsciousness. Nevertheless, Heidegger rejects the traditional idea of epistemological subjectivity. Consequently, Heidegger (1988) downgraded perception to merely "the mode of access to the existent" (p. 49) and rejects the idea that perception and subjectivity should somehow constitute Being.

Therefore, Heidegger (1988, p. 201) also had reservations with regard to the utility of Husserl's epoché and reduction and indicated that Husserl may have confounded essential knowledge with method by allowing the procedure of phenomenological reduction to relegate knowledge to the realm of pure intentionality. Instead, Heidegger (Heidegger and Boss, 2001) argued that while ontological phenomena are "primary in the order of being but secondary in order of being seen" (p. 6), they nevertheless belong together as two aspects of existence.

Consequently, the purpose of the phenomenological reduction should be to elucidate the ontological difference between beings and their Beings, i.e., to execute a reduction that moves the researcher's focus from the ontic phenomena toward the ontological phenomena, but in such a way that beings and their Being are still understood as a union (Marder, 2011). This may seem somewhat vague and confusing, and Heidegger (1988) did admit that "ontological interpretations are more like a groping about than an inquiry clear in its method" (p. 322). Nevertheless, the following will attempt to clarify the method from the perspective of the foundational literature.

Beingness and Concepts

According to Heidegger, the central concern of each of the sciences is an ontological preoccupation with beingness (Craig, 2019) because science is essentially an act of Being with the world. Therefore, due to Dasein's comportment, all objects have a particular meaningfulness, which gives them a certain identity and in turn allows them to belong to categories of things. Thus, in *Being and Time*, Heidegger (2010) argued that "the totality of beings can with respect to its various domains, become the field where particular domains of knowledge are exposed and delimited," such as "history, nature, space, life, human being, language and so on" (p. 8). Heidegger (1988) further clarified his position in the 1927 lectures titled *The Basic Problem of Phenomenology*, where he stated that all "sciences have as their theme some Being or Beings" (p. 13).

Thus, Being can be understood as the delimitation of specific domains of knowledge that originate from Dasein's interpretations of the world, and which actualize in abstract concepts. Here we can see an outline of a particular type of phenomenological research that takes aim at revising the meaning of concepts, constructs, and terminology through Dasein analysis (i.e., Dasein's comportment or dealings with things in the world; Heidegger, 1988, p.318). In this manner,

Dasein analysis has an agenda similar to that of the Dutch School of phenomenological psychology but relies on an entirely different theoretical framework.

The assumptions are that Dasein is not conceptually aware of the distinction between beings and Being when it is immersed in its worldly doings and dealings. Dasein's understanding of Being is therefore mostly latent and "the ontological difference" (Heidegger, 1988, p. 319) requires interpretation. Since Dasein's comportment (i.e., care is in order to and for the sake of) is therefore temporal, the interpretative horizon is temporality (Dreyfuss, 1995, p. 244). Thus, Heidegger stated that Dasein's temporal projection upon situations as possibilities of what has been and what can be is how Dasein objectifies Being and accomplishes the "conceptualizability" (p. 323) of Being. Consequently, Heidegger (1988) argued that "all propositions of ontology are temporal propositions" (p. 323) "about being in the light of time" (p. 324).

In this way, Heidegger (1988) quoted Plato, stating, "The ascent to Being from the depths of beings, by means of conceptual thought of the essence, has the character of the recollection of something already previously seen" (p. 326). In other words, the formulation of concepts as well as their revisions is based on an interpretation of something that is already latently understood from how Dasein relates to things. Just think of the concepts in common law. They are all codifications of what is already latently understood as true and right where the logic of judicial argumentation relies on the interpretation of precedence. Therefore, it establishes the identity of the case and its belonging to categories of similar cases and subsequently an examination of how judges and juries related to those cases in the past.

In other words, a ruling on a specific case is in a manner of speaking an "objectification of what has somehow already been unveiled beforehand" (Heidegger, 1988, p. 320).

In this connection, Heidegger (2010) argued that scientific progress takes place when we force ourselves "to ask questions of the basic constitution of each domain" (p. 8), and the "real movement of the sciences takes place in the revision of basic concepts" (p. 9). To this end, Heidegger proposed what can be conceived as a three-step method for the analysis of Dasein, which includes (a) reduction, (b) construction, and (c) destruction.

Phenomenological Reduction

Heidegger (1988) reinterpreted Husserl's concept of reduction to mean a method of "leading phenomenological vision back from the

apprehension of a being, whatever may be the character of that apprehension to the understanding of the Being of this being" (p. 21). The
reduction is essentially hermeneutic because the researcher must move
beyond merely describing the ontic (what appears) and instead conceive the ontically present as a clue that ultimately leads to its ontological ground (Spiegelberg, 1971, p. 695). For example, Heidegger (2010)
argued that "the structure of being of what is at hand as a useful thing
is determined by reference" (p. 74) and these references are essentially
"the in-order-to to a what-for" (p. 74). However, Heidegger recognized
that the reduction alone will not make Being stand out from beings.
Essentially, the reduction is here a mental preparation, where reflection on the ontological difference becomes a clearing that allows Being
to be grasped relative to time. Heidegger, therefore, proposes that the
reduction must be accompanied by a complimentary move:

Phenomenological Construction

Here we lean into Being by freely projecting upon things and situations
the "factual experiences of beings and the range of possibilities of
experience that at any time are peculiar to a factical Dasein" (Heidegger,
1988, p. 22). In this manner, the construction of Being becomes a task
of interpreting things and situations in the light of time. As noted earlier, Dasein is temporal and in a sense historical, and therefore
Heidegger argued that "possibilities of access and modes of interpretation of beings are themselves diverse, varying in different historical
circumstances" (p. 22). As an example, Heidegger elaborated on his
own studies of Being and pointed out how other philosophers through
time conceptualized Being and how this history of conceptual possibilities of Being allowed him to objectify Being from a temporal horizon
and reinterpret an already existing concept of Being. In this manner,
Heidegger does not construct the concept of Being from his own direct
experience with beings. Instead, the Dasein that he himself is allows for
a much broader horizon than just his own limited experience horizon.

The Phenomenological Destruction

In light of the second move, Heidegger argued that "there necessarily
belongs to the conceptual interpretation of Being and its structures"
(p. 22) "a destruction," which is a critical process in which the traditional concepts, which at first must necessarily be employed are decon-
structed down to the source from which they are drawn" (p. 23). We
are here not talking about a rejection of historical concepts, but more

of an appropriation of these. Heidegger's own writing is an instructive example of this, as his conceptualization of Being and the meaning of Being always takes its starting point from the clarification and reinterpretation of thinkers such as Plato, Hegel, Kant, et cetera. In this manner, as Heidegger already knows what he is looking for (i.e., the ontological difference), he appropriates a new conceptualization of Being in terms of temporality through a simultaneous process of historical construction and deconstruction of this concept.

Identity and Being

We could perhaps have left it at this, but Boss (2000) saw a great potential in Heidegger's phenomenology for clarifying the concept of the subject and invited Heidegger to dialogue with him and other practitioners on how existential phenomenology could be applied to the practice of psychotherapy. Although the purpose of Boss's Dasein analytics was to improve the theoretical foundation of psychotherapy, the attempt at naturalizing Heidegger's phenomenology may inform research as well as therapy.

Dasein is not an ego, but a form of publicness constituted in temporality. Boss (2000, p. 217) therefore pointed out that the main challenge in Dasein analytics of the human being is to avoid falling prey to Freudian metaphysical concepts. Instead, Boss (1982) argued that we should focus on understanding Dasein's "Being-ness" (p. 37), and the first step is to accept the idea that Being-ness is not a characteristic of Dasein. Being-ness is Dasein itself. In other words, Dasein does not exist in-itself (p. 40) like Husserl's conceptualization of the transcendental subject or Freud's ego.

Dasein only exists in its relating to the world, in its being with and care for things in the world. It is therefore Dasein's behavior that discloses Being-ness of the world and of itself. This is somewhat of an uncomfortable position since we are accustomed to excusing our bad behaviors with statements such as, "This is not who I am." However, the behavior is exactly the "am" of the "who." Thus, Dasein only exists in the mode of relating to something and always loses itself to the particular things and situations it relates to. Consequently, Boss (1982, p. 42) argued that the "human being and what appears in the light of human existence are mutually dependent on each other," and it is from this conceptualization of the human subject Dasein analysis must begin. In this way, the researcher may achieve essential insights about Dasein's Being-ness by investigating Dasein's "existentialia" and "temporality" (Boss, 1982, p. 47).

Analysis of Dasein's Existentialia

Heidegger (2002, p. 31) argued that "man is essentially this relationship of responding to being and he is only this," and therefore "man remains referred to being and so answers to it" (p. 31). This insight led Boss (1982) to argue that Dasein's existentialia are "nothing other than the very meaning and essence of directly observable human behaviour" (p. 40). Consequently, the task is to elucidate the essence of Dasein in terms of a "rule in relation to what it encounters" (p. 41). This means that the notion of "lived experience" must be reinterpreted as how Dasein typically copes and deals with the situations it encounters.

However, due to the publicness of Dasein, we are not concerned with the psychological coping mechanisms of the individual but with the averageness of "copingness" that belongs to the "they-self." Therefore, Heidegger's insight that "Dasein understands itself as a rule in relation to what it encounters" (Boss, 1982 p. 40) becomes a question pertaining to "they-self." Thus, Heidegger (2001a, p. 8E) explained that although Dasein is not a subject or an ego, "Dasein is an entity that determines itself as I am. ... Dasein is therefore also my Dasein," but because Dasein is also constituted in "being with," Heidegger argued that it is not I myself who for the most part and on average am my Dasein, but the Others" and that "no one is himself in everydayness."

In other words, to understand Dasein as a "rule" with regard to what it encounters is to question interpreting Dasein from the perspective of traditions, history, and the way things are usually done. Thus, Heidegger (2001a) stated, "I myself is to a certain extent that which I deal with, that with which I occupy myself, that to which my profession chains me, and in these my Dasein takes place" (p. 9E). Thus, Dasein is a happening, which means that the situations that Dasein encounters should not be described in terms of "what" but rather in terms of the "how" (p. 13E). Thus Heidegger (2002) argued, "[T]he event of appropriation," which is "the essence of identity," (p. 39) emerges from the interpretation of "human behaviour" (Boss, 1982, p. 40), but not because a situation impacts Dasein or shapes Dasein. Dasein simply is the action, and therefore, "it is not about the content, about what we are doing, it is about how we do it" (Koloskov, 2022). In other words, identity determines Being and Being is therefore a characteristic of identity and not the other way around (Heidegger, 2002, p. 28).

Koloskov (2022) articulated this quite poetically by stating that identity is where "one belongs to the others oneself, and entrenches their power" and continues by stating,

> *Das Man* first introduces me into being-in-the-world in the ful-ly-fledged sense of the word: through constant social training I become a member of society; I can do what I am expected to do, I understand the way I am expected to understand. But by doing so, I am firstly really taught how to be *someone* as such and what is at stake for this someone.

"I can be myself only because I am just another other, that is, because I do not differentiate myself from others for the most part but tacitly accept the relentless dictate of the one."

Analysis of Dasein's Temporality

Craig (2019, p. 39) argued that Heidegger's work uncovered several universal characteristics of Dasein. Hereunder, (a) "That we are thrown into a time and culture"; (b) "we fall in with our culture and time and largely exist as an inauthentic they-self"; (c) that we exist in time from birth to death. Heidegger (1988) thus stated,

> Hence there arises the prospect of a possible confirmation of the thesis that [t]ime is the horizon from which something like Being becomes at all intelligible. We interpret Being by way of time. The interpretation is a temporal one. The fundamental subject of research in ontology, as determination of the meaning of being by way of time, is *Temporality*.
>
> (p. 16-17)

In this manner, Dasein is open to the possibilities of doings and dealings that the past, present, and future offer up as possibilities. This explains the phenomenon where individuals form enduring identities around events that they themselves may never have participated in or no longer participate in or even wish to someday participate in. Thus, according to Boss (2000), Dasein chooses what in time and space it cares about and stated that we are free to choose "which of our possi-bilities we will carry out, into which of our possibilities we will allow ourselves to become absorbed" (p. 222).

In this connection, Heidegger (2010) argued that "when one understands oneself projectively in an existentiell possibility, the future underlies this understanding and it does so as a coming-to-ward-oneself from the actual possibility as which Dasein in each instances exists" (p. 321). Boss (1982, p. 48) therefore stated that "man's whole future waits for him. Until the moment of his death new possibilities for world disclosures approaches him from his future possibilities, which must be taken over, whose fulfilment he still owes" (p. 321). Thus, Heidegger made a salient observation that sets Dasein analysis apart from the Husserlian method. In Heidegger's (1968) view, it is not primarily what "actuality strikes man" (p. 9) in the form of perceptions that we need to concern ourselves with, but rather what eludes the individual (i.e., the fulfillment of our possibilities of becoming that are always just around the corner). Our entire comportment is toward such fulfillment. Thus, Dasein's comportment is a gesture that points, and whatever points is a sign, and therefore Heidegger (1968) stated, "[W]e are a sign that is not read" (p. 18).

Methodological Considerations

The aforementioned elaborations on Dasein's existentialia and temporality are obviously two sides of the same coin, and one cannot come to an understanding of Dasein's Being from only a static presentation of Dasein's existentialia because time is the horizon of interpretation. In this manner, the elucidation of Dasein's being is not a psychological investigation but remains ontological because we are essentially trying to clarify what the human being is. Boss (2000, p. 222) therefore argued that in Dasein analysis, "our primary concern is with those potentialities, capacities or possibilities that constitute Da-sein, the human being" because understanding the "who" of Dasein is always what is at stake when we interpret our subjects' pursuit of their possibilities (Koloskov, 2022).

From the previous elaboration, it is now clear that identity and being are projections of possibilities in time (Javorská, 2016) and that individuals choose events in the present, the past, as well as from an envisioned future as challenge frameworks, which allow them to come face-to-face with their own Being. In other words, "we exist as a bundle of possibilities for relating to the world" (Boss, 2000, p. 222), and therefore we must consider our research subjects' disclosures as "appeals to be" (Craig, 2019, p. 52) rather than accounts of what happened to them in the past.

In this manner, we could say that Being is Dasein's conceptual idea of its own identity as a possibility. However, this idea is still latent and in need of elucidation. Hence, the methodological steps considered in the previous section – reduction, construction, and destruction – are still applicable and should be applied in order not to fall prey to psychologizing.

The Research Domain of Anthropological Phenomenology

Both Heidegger and Sartre were existentialists, and what these two thinkers have in common is the notion that existence precedes essence. However, Sartre's and Heidegger's conceptualizations of existence, and hereunder, the phenomenon of the human being is quite different. Thus, when Heidegger (1988, p. 65) spoke of Dasein, he was not referring to an actual human being, but rather to an existential comportment or a form of behavior toward the world, which he referred to as care, and it is from caring that both the Being of the world and Dasein's Being comes to be understood.

However, Dasein only knows the ways of caring that everyone else is caring and mainly cares about the same things that everyone else cares about. Therefore, the Being that comes to Dasein's understanding is a form of publicness, where Dasein is extrapolating its being from the possibilities that are already available. Consequently, Dasein's operational self is a they-self outside of its authentic self. Thus, in his response to Sartre's (2007) 1945 lecture on existentialism, Heidegger (1977, p. 206) stated that in his view, "existence means standing out into the truth of being" or a state of perpetual "revealing-revealed." In this manner, Sartre (1992) argued that Heidegger stayed true to his maxims by avoiding "any appeal to consciousness in his description of Dasein" (p. 134).

In response, Sartre found that Heidegger's conceptualization of Dasein was haunted by a latent self because by the notion that Dasein understands Being, Sartre found that Heidegger re-established "the dimension of consciousness." Sartre (1992) thus argued that "understanding has meaning only if it is consciousness of understanding" (p. 134). While Heidegger (1988) found the notion of a consciousness that can climb out of itself over to the objects an "absurdity" (p. 64), Sartre (1992) thought that while consciousness in-itself may not be able to do so because it is just "a background of pure appearances" (p. 17), then consciousness accomplishes this climb through self-consciousness.

In this manner, Sartre bridges Husserlian and Heideggerian phenomenology by on the one hand acknowledging that our lifeworld is constituted in human subjectivity but on the other hand constitution does not take place in the passivity of givenness, but through the small and large projects that we choose to engage with (Spiegelberg, 1971, p. 473). Thus, Sartre's phenomenology acquires a distinct anthropological perspective as we are here focusing on the lives of actual human beings and how they choose to act out in the world. For example, Sartre (1992) explained that if his desired state of affairs is to enjoy a good meal, then "this meal which beyond the dusty road on which I am travelling is projected as the meaning of this road" (p. 614).

We are therefore not positing the world through apperceptions, but instead choosing the desired end goal, acting toward it and revealing the world in accordance with "the end chosen" (p. 614). Consequently, the life world of the ordinary human being is a correlate of free will. These insights give rise to the question of ethics, which was largely ignored by Heidegger, who appeared agnostic toward the inherent value proposition of Being. We can therefore posit that the research domain of Sartre's anthropological phenomenology ultimately becomes human ethics. Thus, Sartre (1992) concluded that "the for-it-self being means to make known to oneself what one is by means of a possibility appearing as a value" and therefore "value haunts the for-itself" (p. 722).

The Research Methods of Anthropological Phenomenology

Sartre agreed with Husserl that consciousness is always being conscious of something, but in contrast to Husserl, Sartre (1992) concluded that this is only possible in the mode of self-consciousness (p. 14). Thus, Sartre (1992) declared Husserl's "hypotheses of the transcendental subject useless" (p. 318) because it effectively requires a splitting of the ego into two, the transcendental and the psychological, where the idea of a transcendental ego would undermine the notion that the Being of the lifeworld is a correlate of free will.

From this follows that there is no "hidden man" behind the curtain that awaits to be revealed by the epoché and reduction. The human being is an organized whole existing in the world, and Sartre (1992) therefore argued that "consciousness is a concrete being *sui generis*, not an abstract unjustifiable relation of identity. It is selfness and not the seat of an opaque, useless ego" (p. 323). Thus, our inherent freedom to choose our own end goals is what illuminates Being (p. 616). Therefore, selfness is "the foundation of personal existence" (p. 323). In other words, where Husserl and Heidegger debate the axiom of "I think therefore I am," Sartre recalibrated this axiom, by positing: I want thus I am (Meagher, 2021).

Consequently, Sartre posited that there is no real distinction between the "choice I make of myself" (p. 709) and the choice I make of my situations, and therefore our being is essentially the ongoing "project of living" (p. 721). Sartre (1992) referred to this phenomenon as the fundamental "project of being or desire of being" (p. 721). From this perspective, our selfness comes to expression in our various projects, which in turn shape our experience of the world in a manner where the world is "experienced as a set of reason for action that reflect our values" (Webber, 2018, p. 114).

In this connection, Sartre (1992) argued that a special phenomenological method is necessary to make the project of living explicit and calls for the development of an "existential psychoanalysis" (p. 617) that remains focused on concrete occurring situations encountered by, for example, "the individual writer or worker" (Spiegelberg, 1971, p. 481). To this end, Sartre proposed the following steps, which can be identified toward the end of *Being and Nothingness*.

Descriptions of Desires and Choices. With a starting point in concrete experiences, the researcher attempts to describe and catalogue concrete desires. These desires are empirically discernible and immanent to the experiences subjects disclose. At the same time, these experiences are also a transcendence of subjectivity and symbolize the constitution of the individual itself (Sartre, 1992, p. 720). In other words, we are not to understand the truth of the human being from the sum of desires and choices but understand that each desire and each choice represents the totality of the human being's ethics.

Thematic Categorizations. Following the cataloguing of desires, the researcher will attempt to establish behavior patterns and types of desires (p. 734). This is accomplished by constant comparison of acts and behaviors so that the researcher can reduce their individual characteristics and circumstances to categories and "fix them conceptually" (p. 726). These categories are manifestations of free will and the reality the individual has chosen to live and thereby also the constituents of "the individual person" (p. 727). In other words, there is no real difference between the reality we have chosen to live in and the person we have chosen to be. Subsequently, the researcher attempts to build an ontology (p. 735) of the individual's project of being by thematizing these categories in terms of, for example, "a taste for adventure, jealousy etc." (p. 726).

Psychoanalytical Interpretation. In the next stage of the analysis, Sartre's method slides from a constitutive ontology of the individual's reality into a form of psychoanalysis. Sartre (1992) described existential psychoanalysis is a hermeneutic method for the purpose of establishing "the human truth of the person" (p. 725). To a certain degree, there is a convergence of goals between Sartre's approach and Dasein analysis interrogation of Being and identity. In addition, both Sartre and Boss draw some inspiration from Freud's psychoanalysis. The main difference would be that Sartre is trying to elucidate the human truth of the person in terms of a value, whereas Dasein analysis is looking for identity. Further, existential psychoanalysis is not trying to elucidate the state of a person based on past experiences nor in this manner to articulate a diagnosis. Instead, the method aims at an elucidation of a person's "original choice" (p. 728).

To assist our understanding of existential psychoanalysis, it may be instructive to first consider how this approach differs from Giorgi's (2009) phenomenological psychological method. To this end, the difference in how they examine jealousy is instructive. Giorgi attempted to describe and understand how jealousy is lived out (p. 156) in order to posit the invariant experiential structures of this concept, which may be generally applicable to more than one person (p. 166). Giorgi (2009) presented a detailed analysis of particular situations, where a subject felt jealous, and through his mitigated psychological reduction, he concluded that an "essential constituent of jealousy" is "that a person desires for herself positive feelings that are going towards another or others" (p. 192). In this manner, Giorgi fulfills the traditional purpose of phenomenological psychology by clarifying the ontology of psychological concepts.

In contrast, Sartre (1992) zooms in on the notion of desire and argued that there is a transcending meaning in jealousy and that this attitude is also an expression of "the choice of myself" (p. 720). In this manner, Sartre (1992) argued,

[A] jealousy of a particular date in which the subject historicizes himself in relation to a certain woman, signifies for the one who knows how to interpret it, the total relation to the world by which the subject constitutes himself as a self.

(p. 720)

Thus, jealousy is a fundamental relation of the self "to the world and to itself (selfness)" (p. 719). Therefore, Sartre (1992) argued jealousy brings about the individual's "community with others, thus making it possible to state that there is a truth concerning man" (p. 724).

However, Sartre's (1992) "self" is, in contrast to the psychological ego, free and therefore can "assume the situation with the proud consciousness of being the author of it" (p. 708) rather than being a passive recipient of exterior circumstances. Thus, Sartre argued that there are "no accidents in a life" because "any way you look at it, it is a matter of a choice" (p. 708). This leads the analysis toward the insight that value "haunts the for-itself" (p. 763) and therefore existential psychoanalysis is, in the final analysis, what Sartre (1992) called "a moral description, for it releases to us the ethical meaning of various human projects."

Drummond (2021) argued that it would be a mistake to think that Sartre's consideration regarding the intersection between selfness, freedom, and ethics is merely mental exercises for phenomenologists, and he pointed to areas where theory and method can be applied – for example, investigations of what it means to be a citizen, the essense of "civil law," and the nature of "justice" (p. 193). Further, we can point to Sartre's own themes (i.e., the encounter with the others), which inform Black and feminist existentialism as well as critical phenomenology.

The Research Domain of Hermeneutic Phenomenology

Ricoeur may not have identified as an existentialist, but he nevertheless took up Heidegger's Dasein as the theme of his study of the constitution of personal identity. However, in contrast to Sartre, Ricoeur seemingly rejected the notion that the self and the world is a correlate of free will as well as Sartre's axiom that identity of the human being is equal to the projects we undertake (Spiegelberg, 1971, p. 568). Instead, he connected hermeneutics with phenomenology as he argued that "human sciences may be said to be hermeneutical inasmuch as their objects display some of the features constitutive of a text, and inasmuch as their methodologies develops the same kind of procedures as those of *Auslegung* or text-interpretation" (Ricoeur, 2019, p. 159).

Thus, Ricoeur (1994) posited that the constitution of personal identity takes place in "speech situations" (p. 329), where a dialectic process between self-designation and the ascription by others plays out in discourse. In this manner, Ricoeur argued that because we emplot ourselves as characters in a narrative, then the characters other people play are necessary for the construal of identities. For example, the role Judas plays in the New Testament is indispensable for providing us with the answer as to who Jesus is, because without a Judas, the story of Jesus could not move forward to its culmination.

In addition, Ricoeur (1994) explained that the constitution of a personal identity is not the product of an ego that posits itself as Sartre argues. Instead, the ego understands who it is from the existence of "the other than self" (p. 329). However, "the other" is not merely a contrast to the self as Judas would be to Jesus. The "other" belongs to the very constitution of personal identity. Thus Ricoeur (2019) stated,

"[W]e ourselves are what the other is" (p. 16) and, therefore, other people are "*a phenomenological modification of myself*" (Moran, 2000, p. 177). For example, Ricoeur (1994) explained that by identifying with a "heroic other" (p. 121) the individual assumes this otherness as its own and internalizes the hero's evaluative preferences, which "defines the moral aspects of character" (p. 122).

Thus, Ricoeur (1994) argued that the hermeneutics of the self is the determination of selfhood by its confrontation with sameness (p. 116) and "its dialectic with otherness" (p. 297), and personal identity is brought into view through the individual's attestations of evaluative preferences in speech situations. In this manner, personal identity comes to involve "the same narrative understanding as the plot itself" (p. 143). Consequently, Ricoeur (1994) called for a different kind of phenomenology "of the self, affected by the other than self" (p. 33) to elucidate the constitutive role of otherness and discourse for personal identity. Indeed, this is the theme that Ricoeur explores in his seminal work *Oneself as Another*, first published in 1990.

The Research Methods of Hermeneutic Phenomenology

The aforementioned elaboration should have clarified that the research domain of hermeneutic phenomenology is selfhood and personal identity, and in this light, we should understand Ricoeur's hermeneutic method. In other words, the purpose of the methodological consideration in the following is to understand persons better than they understand themselves (i.e., "beyond the limited horizon" of their own existential situations; Ricoeur, 2019, p. 147).

This statement might provoke qualitative researchers who rely on in-group verification or member check for validation of research findings, but to illuminate the constitution of personal identity as a phenomenon, we must avoid embracing standpoint epistemology. We are here engaged in an exploration of Dasein and not in reproducing the self-identification of a particular individual. In this connection, we must reiterate that Dasein comports in the mode of the "they self" (Heidegger, 2010, p. 303), which means that Dasein in its everydayness tends to "understand itself in terms of the world taken care of" (p. 307) or the projects it engages in. Consequently, Heidegger argued that "the being that we ourselves in each case are, is ontologically farthest from us" (p. 297) and therefore requires "an ontological interpretation" (p. 298).

The data we work with are verbal disclosures emerging from the discourse between subjects and researcher. In this connection, Heidegger (1977) stated,

> Language is the house of Being. In its home man dwells. Those who think and those who create with words are the guardians of this home. Their guardianship accomplishes the manifestation of Being insofar as they bring the manifestation to language and maintain it in language through their speech.
>
> (p. 217)

However, Heidegger (2010) pointed out that the "natural talk about the I take place in the they-self" (p. 307). Therefore, "what expresses itself in the I is that self which, initially and for the most part, I am not authentically" (p. 307) and when Dasein comports through speech and language (Heidegger & Boss, 2001, p. 16), this disclosure is not private; it is, so to speak, "unowned."

In this connection, Ricoeur (2019) introduced a form of hermeneutic epoché, which he referred to as distanciation. This move has two moments, also referred to as double hermeneutics. The first move is oriented toward the individual's sense of self in the speech situation. The subsequent move is an attempt at interpreting this sensemaking from the perspective of social, cultural, and other references in an individual's verbal disclosures, which imply the symbolic presence of otherness. The distinction between the first and second move in fact mirrors Husserl's notion of active and passive syntheses, where speech is active and language is passive.

In the first move, the researchers bracket the everydayness and commonness of their subjects' disclosures so that they no longer take an interest in whether the content is factual or not. Hence, they reduce their subjects' speech to the phenomenon of speech-acts (pp. 76–77), where they focus on "who is speaking, who is acting, who is recounting about him or herself and who is the moral subject" (Ricoeur, 1994, p. 16). They do not conceive of these disclosures as recalls of lived experiences. Instead, they conceive of these speech-acts as attestations of self. Thus, Ricoeur (1994) argued that the question of "who?" is preserved and can be identified at every level of "self-attestation," hereunder "linguistic, praxis, narrative, and prescriptive. Consequently, Ricoeur (1994) argued that "the decisive step in the direction of a narrative conception of personal identity is taken" (p. 143) when the researcher allows action to signify character. In other, words we are not attempting to "live or relive" our subjects' experiences. Instead, we "interrupt lived experience in order to signify it" (Ricoeur, 2019, p. 76).

The second distanciation move puts the attestations and speech into question, where we consider how the narrative expresses a belonging to a particular cultural and historical tradition. In this way, Scheler (2009) argued that the human being is unique in the sense that it is capable of detaching from its physical situatedness and transforming apperceptions of its own existence into a "symbol" (p. 28) world that finds its expression in discourse. Thus, the self uses symbols and internalizes these as values, which in turn attests to a cultural and historical belonging. Thus, Scheler (1954) argued that "not only is the "I" a member of the "we" but also the "we" is a necessary member of the "I" (p. 230) because we live most of our lives through our communities rather than our egos and, in addition, "anything in our experience which can be put into words is always something which, having been singled out by common language, must also be accessible to others" (p. 252). Hence, the purpose of the second distanciation is to "interrupt the relation of belonging in order to signify it" (Ricoeur, 2019, p. 77).

Nørreklit (2006) used the following allegory to illustrate the hermeneutic moves. He compared the subject's self-consciousness to a house that the narrative self has built for its selfness to live in that protects it from the randomness of life by providing structure and a "safe space of meaning" (p. 5). However, as Ricoeur (1994) pointed out, "consciousness is in truth, that place par excellence in which illusions about oneself is intimately bound up with the veracity of attestation" (p. 341).

Therefore, it is not enough for the researcher to describe the structures of the house. The researcher also needs to understand why the house is built in the way it is. In this connection, Ricoeur (1994) suggested that Freudian psychoanalysis and other lenses that challenge the illusion the house represents could be productive interpretative techniques (Langdridge, 2008). Scott-Baumann (2012, p. 60) characterized this move as a "hermeneutics of suspicion," where the researchers' theoretical perspectives and prior knowledge challenge their subjects' narratives in the same way therapists challenge delusions during psychoanalysis and argued that this is indeed "an integral part of an appropriation of meaning" (p. 68).

From this follows that the hermeneutic researcher truly is the main instrument of research, and Ricoeur (2019) explained that the final step of meaning appropriation means to "make one's own what was initially alien" (p. 145). In this manner, the understanding of who the other is and the understanding of oneself do not have firm delimitation. Scheler (1954) thus argued that "understanding is not confined to the understanding of others." "It is equally ultimately an understanding of oneself" (p. 224).

Review of the Existential Phenomenological Research Literature

In principle, we are in the business of investigating Dasein and not subjectivity. However, these conceptualizations of the human being are often confounded in applied research, especially in IPA studies, which actually make a methodological point out of conflating Husserl and Heidegger's very different takes on phenomenology (see Eatough & Smith, 2017). For example, researching the implications of childhood behavioral patterns for managers facing critical situations, Müller et al. (2022a) specifically invoked Boss's Dasein analysis but lumps his approach together with Binswanger's Dasein analytics, which both Boss and Heidegger viewed as resting on a subjectivist misconception of Dasein (Boss, 1982, p. 51). Heidegger (Heidegger & Boss, 2001) specifically stated during the Zollikon Seminars that Binswanger "misunderstood the analytic of Dasein" (p. 115) and that this form of subjectivism "blocks clear insight into the phenomenological hermeneutrics of Dasein" (p. 120). Consequently, Müller et al.'s (2022a) analysis moved toward what can best be described as a genetic phenomenological analysis as they conceived childhood experiences as constituents of the subjects' behaviors in critical situations. However, this study still contradicts the axioms of Husserlian phenomenology as the researchers transgressed into psychologism by proposing a conceptual model of how childhood experiences impact failures in career development later on in life.

Further, Müller et al. (2022b) studied how managers make sense of crisis situations and argued that the phenomenological domain is intersubjectivity, but the interpretation is rooted in Dasein analysis. While Heidegger (2002) argued that crisis situations can be considered as frameworks, where the human being is forced to confront Being (p. 35), then a closer reading of their methodology revealed that rather than interpreting the data from the perspective of Dasein's existentialia and temporality, they imposed an extant theoretical framework. The concepts of the external theory were applied deductively for categorizing the interview data, and thereby Müller et al. (2022b) inadvertently allowed the themes of the extant theory to take priority over Dasein. Consequently, the result of this study becomes a conceptual framework that posits a theory of how managers make sense of crisis and what career choices they subsequently make.

The methodological problem is that no reduction is applied, which means that we remain focused on the beings, and the study never considers the ontological difference pertaining to their Being. It can therefore be argued that in this and several other IPA studies, Heidegger is invoked more as a totem than putting his theory of Dasein to work. Indeed, it is the absence of the reduction that makes IPA research so incompatible with phenomenological theory.

So where do we find research that truly examines Dasein in the reduction? First, we must accept the axiom that when we examine Dasein, we reject the conceptualization of the human being as "subjectivity and as transcendental ego-consciousness" (Heidegger and Boss, 2001, p. 120). Where phenomenological researchers struggle to escape the psychologism that, for example, Müller et al. (2022a, 2022b) embedded in their studies, I would suggest that we instead turn our attention to the emerging field of social media research.

In this connection, Lagerkvist (2017) posited what Heidegger referred to as Dasein's thrownness into an already existing world, which manifests on social media as "the thrownness of digital human existence" (p. 96). Due to the nature of social media where personality and body no longer present as a synthesis, it can be argued that Lagerkvist (2017) is by default examining Dasein. Thus, on social media, researchers are confronted with data from the agglomeration of multiple personalities, which presents as a "the they." "The nobody whom the everyday Dasein has always surrendered itself" (Heidegger, 2010, p. 124).

Thus, in netnographic research (online ethnography), we are from the very beginning operating in the reduction. For example, Wang's (2020) study *The Digital Dasein of Chinese Rural Migrants* documented how migrants experienced a sense of being "un-persons" due to their isolation from the communities, where they were physically located. In response, they developed virtual relationships, where they assumed the identity of a "desired self" by posting images of idealized models instead of their own authentic selves. This was not a case of misleading others by pretending to be someone else because their online connections know and share the same migrant realities. Thus, Wang (2020) concluded that the image postings represented a shared aspirational reality of rural migrant workers, where Dasein is projecting itself upon possibilities to be. However, possibilities are inherently commercialized and inauthentic or a case of oneself as another.

Staying with the social media theme, Asthana (2017) applied Ricoeur's narrative approach in the study of social media postings of Palestinian youths from the Westbank. The researcher conceived of the posted videos and images as a "text" and submitted them to a hermeneutic analysis. In this manner, Asthana (2017) demonstrated that these youths used social media to convert their vulnerability into a narrative of resilience and resistance that "constituted aspects of their youth refugee selfhood" (p. 107). Although the outcome of this study speaks to the phenomenon of selfhood, which is central to Ricoeur's phenomenology, the applied methods reflected generic qualitative techniques such as data categorization, rather than the hermeneutic methods proposed by Ricoeur (2019).

In contrast, Fredholm et al.'s (2019) study of medical students' experiences of feeling like a doctor demonstrated a more deliberate involvement with Ricoeur's phenomenology, as the topic of the research invoked the themes from *Oneself as Another*. In addition, Fredholm et al. (2019) were aware of Ricoeur's distanciation technique as their analysis moved "from what the text says towards what it talks about" (p. 116). To this end, they allowed the preunderstandings of the researchers and self-determination theory to function as tools of hermeneutic suspicion that, according to Scott-Baumann (2012), "seeks to discover a hidden reality operative under appearances" (p. 66). Consequently, Fredholm et al.'s (2019) findings appeared more as a product of the hermeneutic methodology than those of Asthana's (2017).

Anthropological phenomenology is an approach that is rarely encountered in applied research, but Parker's (2015) book *Sartre and No Child Left Behind: An Existential Psychoanalytic Anthropology of Urban Schooling* is an instructive example. The perspective on the constitution of the self and the lifeworld is aligned with Sartre's emphasis on choice and free will, but like Sartre, Parker acknowledged that the choices of the individual are limited by the choices of those in power, who can choose the situations the less powerful have to contend with. Hence Parker (2015) zoomed in on the policy choices that have shaped the public education options available for Black communities. Consequently, his examination of urban education raised the question of what role these choices play in the students becoming who they are. In this manner, his study acquired the ethical dimension that sets Sartre's phenomenology apart from Husserl and Heidegger.

On the other hand, Parker appeared to already understand the nature of the problem afflicting schools in Black communities and, in this manner, it appears as if Sartre's theories were used more for heuristic purposes than for facilitating an outcome that is not already known. However, with this approach, Parker emphasized that the situations Black students find themselves in are a matter of choice, just not their own. In this manner, Parker builds a bridge from Sartre's anthropological phenomenology to critical phenomenology, which is the theme of the following chapter.

9   Critical Phenomenology

In Part 4 of *Being and Nothingness*, Sartre (1992) argued that the self and its lifeworld do not solely arise out of the ends the individual pursues, but that three layers of reality intersect to constitute the situation of the individual (p. 654): (a) instrumental phenomena that already have meanings such as tools, institutions and culture; (b) my persona, hereunder race, sex, gender, nationality, physical appearance, and abilities; (c) other people as points of reference. In this manner, the individual finds itself in a world of meanings that are not constituted within the first person's point of view but are pregiven. Thus Sartre (1992) stated, "I find myself engaged in an already meaningful world which reflect to me meanings which I have not put into it" (p. 655).

From this follows that the self is not only a product of the end it chooses but as much a product of the avenues of choice made available. For example, paperwork upon which our lives depend such as identity documents, marriage certificates, and voting cards, must be acquired and filled out in certain ways. These artifacts allow us to participate in social life; they provide us with benefits, but they also limit our freedom and can be used to disrupt our personal projects and deprive us of what is necessary to accomplish the ends we have chosen (see Sartre, 1992, p. 656). Consequently, institutions and the others modify the constitution of Being by limiting individual freedom.

Marder (2014) argued that phenomenology becomes critical when we question "the interaction between phenomena and logos" (p. 2) From this perspective, it can be argued that this book is already part of a critical phenomenological tradition as its arc plays on "the phenomenological fissures, divisions, splits, rifts and separations" (p. 5) that have come to characterize the investigation into the problem of constitution.

DOI: 10.4324/9781003270058-9

However, Scheler (1954, p. 220) pointed out a salient problem that gnaws on the bones of the human sciences: that knowledge can "only be taken seriously with reference to educated Northern Europeans of the present day," and in this manner, Scheler foreshadowed the emergence of critical phenomenology, which rejects that social research can be neutral when it comes to race and gender. The epiphany that leads a researcher toward critical phenomenology is that the observer is always embodied, and consequently, there can be no such thing as a point of view from a perspective that is not embodied (see Davidson, 2016, p. 162). Therefore, the requirements that the researchers should be objective and neutral during the inductive procedures serve only to exclude female and Black embodied epistemologies by relegating these perspectives to a form of bias contradictive of the scientific method.

Critical phenomenologists argue that social research tends to reproduce a particular White male point of view, as research remains captive of methodologies grounded in this epistemology. Thus, they reject the notion that the body is just a container for the first-person point of view. The first-person point of view is entirely embodied, and therefore the body's biological and racial attributes mediate between world and mind (Simonsen & Koefod, 2020, p. 7). Critical phenomenology, therefore, draws from phenomenological thinkers such as Merleau-Ponty, de Beauvoir, and Fanon, who shared an interest in the embodied experience (p. 8).

Thus, de Beauvoir and Fanon took their starting point in Sartre's work and opened phenomenology to feminist and Black existential perspectives on the constitutive role of what Sartre referred to as the third ontological dimension of the body. In addition, these thinkers considered how phenomenology could be applied as a method to expunge the female and Black self from this inauthentic being-for-the-other that Sartre identified.

Feminist Phenomenology

Bergoffen (2018) explained that de Beauvoir was critical of the abstractness of phenomenological literature of her time, which did not consider "the historical, economic, sexed, gendered conditions that impact peoples' lives" (p. 326). Consequently, here articulation of feminist phenomenology became infused with both Marxist and existential thought. Thus, she found that Marx's concept of "alienated labor" (p. 327) described the situation women find themselves in as responsible for the bulk of unpaid housework and in this manner a gendered proletariat with the patriarchy constituting the oppressive class.

In contrast to Marxism, de Beauvoir shared Sartre's existential perspective that selfness is a correlate of free will. However, de Beauvoir pointed out that the consequences of Sartre's (2007) axiom that "man is not only that he conceives himself to be, but that which he wills himself to be" (p. 22) is that man wins as "the world becomes present with his presence in it" (Arp, 2005 p. 397). For example, de Beauvior (2015) noted that, within academia, men listen to female scholars in "polite indifference" (p. 18) knowing that their ideas are mere reproductions of ideas men have already determined to be valid. Therefore, men control what is normal, neutral, and objective.

Ultimately, de Beauvoir's agenda is not the liberation of women as a class, and she finds what she referred to as the American obsession with superiority and inferiority of gender categories a distraction from the problem of accomplishing authentic selfhood. Consequently, feminist phenomenology is critical in the sense that it focuses on how women can participate in the generation and transmission of knowledge, how women acquire pathic knowledge, and how women can oppose oppression of their pursuit of their own ends (p. 51). From this, we can see the contours of two research agendas. One that takes aim at women's role in academia and another that takes aim at society in general.

Black Phenomenology

Modern science has largely concluded that what we perceive as race is of no biological significance, but race nevertheless remains a very real phenomenon that appears to broadly determine a person's socioeconomic station in life. This has led to the conclusion that race is a social construct. Within this train of thought, proponents of critical race theory (CRT) emphasize race as a sociological fact and that social, cultural, legal institutions are organized in a manner that reproduces a hierarchical subordination of Black people reminiscent of the early Eurocentric pseudo-biological classification of races. Indeed, this appeared to be the perspective Guenther (2020) assumed, when she advocated for a critical phenomenology that reflects on the "quasi-transcendental social structures" (p. 12) that "influence our capacity to experience the world, not just in isolated instances but in a way that is deeply constitutive of who we are and how we make sense of things" (p. 13). Thus, Davies (2020) concluded that "transcendental subjectivity must be redescribed in terms of intersectionality" of "race, gender and class" (p. 3).

The problem with this perspective is that intersectionality introduces a form of objectivism to the problem of constitution that ultimately must be examined from within the first-person point of view to remain phenomenological. It is therefore important to keep in mind that a phenomenological study of "who we are" is distinct from CRT because we do not take our starting point in the pseudo-facticity of established racial identities because these are ideal objects or concepts that are not immanent to consciousness but belong to what Heidegger referred to as "Das Man." Instead, phenomenologists examine the lived experience of the racialization of the embodied self from the "micro-interactions" (Alcoff, 1999, p. 17) between the self and the other than self.

In this manner, Black critical phenomenology turns away from Husserl's phenomenology as well as from CRT and instead focuses on the interrogation of Sartre's (1992) "third ontological dimension of the body" (p. 460) in the context of postcolonial and White majority societies. Thus, Franz Fanon's seminal work *Black Skin White Masks* (first published in 1952) connected Sartre's existential phenomenology with Black existentialism for the purpose of studying what Fanon refers to as the Black problem. This is not primarily a problem of oppression and marginalization, but a problem concerning the constitution of an authentic selfhood while trapped between two racialized cultures.

In this connection, Fanon (2008) stated, "The white man is locked in his whiteness. The black man in his blackness" (p. xiii), and by this, he meant that these binary categories are a form of "double narcissism" (p. xiv) that disrupts our possibilities for constitution of an authentic self. Thus, Fanon believed that the "juxtaposition of the black and white races has resulted in a massive psycho-existential complex" that requires an investigation of the "various mental attitudes the black man adopts in the face of white civilization" (p. xvi).

The Methods of Critical Phenomenology

The questions of race, gender, ableness, etc., are the subject matter of different sociological and psychological schools, and quite often researchers base their investigations on data gathered from the first-person point of view. However, Oksala (2022) argued that effective social critique demands more than just a thematic presentation of first-person lived experiences and that "some version of the phenomenological reduction should be recognized as indispensable" (p. 2) in order for the critique to reach beyond the existential context of the individual.

Thus, Fanon proposed that what we today would call a critical phenomenological analysis is psychological, regressive, and conducted from the perspective of temporality. These characteristics indicate that

Fanon's analysis takes place within the natural standpoint and the life-world. In addition, Fanon referred to Freud's psychoanalysis. While Freud was indeed a source of inspiration for Fanon (2008), his analysis of "the Being of the Black man" (p. xvii) is more aligned with the "phenomenological psychological tradition" (Desai, 2022. p. 77). Especially the introduction to *Black Skin White Masks* alluded to genetic phenomenology, as Fanon (2008) casually referred to his approach, as a form of psychological "sociodiagnostics" and introduces "sociegeny" (p. xv) as the phenomenon constitutive of Black Being. By sociegeny Fanon meant that the natural attitude of the Black man is "partly formed at the nexus of social structures" (Maldonado-Torres, 2022, p. 91) and not only a question of private mental constitution.

Fanon's purpose was to leverage the phenomenological method to conduct a regressive analysis of the natural attitude of the Black man to expose internalized myths, prejudices, and sedimented attitudes that constitutes his Being. For Fanon as well as de Beauvoir, the aim was not primarily to litigate the narrative of social superiority, inferiority, or equality, but to "desalinate" the conscious mind from the constitutive hegemony of "the other" so that the individual can emerge as an authentic self in its own right as a Being leaning into the future rather than the past. Thus, Fanon (2008) stated, "I am not a prisoner of history. I must not look for the meaning of my destiny in that direction" (p. 204), and "the black man is not. No more than the white man. Both have to move away from the inhumane voices of their respective ancestors so that genuine communication can be born" (p. 205). Hence, the project of critical phenomenology is ultimately not one of race or gender but of humanism.

While neither Fanon's nor de Beauvoir's writing directly invoked genetic phenomenology, there is an argument that this is an appropriate methodology for critical phenomenology. It is not clear to what degree these thinkers were exposed to Husserl's writings from his genetic period, but through their perspectives on embodiment, they would have been familiar with Merleau-Ponty's writing, and in the preface to *Phenomenology of Perception*, he stated that "Husserl in his last works mentions a genetic phenomenology" (1978, p. viii) and further posited "consciousness itself as a project of the world" (p. xx) and therefore "phenomenology can become a phenomenology of origins" because we are no longer only focused on appearances but also consider the entire historical context of phenomena.

Genetic phenomenology is an approach that is largely overlooked in the recent literature about critical phenomenological methods. This is likely because Husserl's works such as *Experience and Judgment* and

Crisis appear alien to the frame of reference of most critical phenomenologists. For example, Guenther's (2020) and Davies's (2020) preoccupation with what essentially is the natural standpoint ought to lead toward a genetic phenomenological method that takes its starting point in the natural attitude and then applies a regressive analysis for the purpose of unbuilding (Abbau) this standpoint into its "formative elements" (Alves, 2021, p. 209). However, the relevant foundational literature that speaks to genetic phenomenology is typically not referenced.

Similarly, Rodemeyer (2020) acknowledged that de Beauvoir's approach "begins with a natural attitude" (p. 240) and thus argued that "Husserl's method of beginning in the natural attitude" is "informative for critical approaches" focused on race and gender. However, without the proper reference to Husserl's later works, Rodemeyer missed the point of the genetic phenomenological analysis and instead entangled his narrative with Husserl's static phenomenological epoché and reduction from *Ideas*.

The problem with invoking Husserl's transcendental methods is that the existential tradition that de Beauvoir and Fanon build from largely rejects the transcendental method. Specifically, Sartre (1992) found the phenomenological reduction "useless and disastrous" (p. 318) because it reduces the problem of constitution to just the first-person perspective. Thus, informed by genetic phenomenology and existentialism, the following steps may form the basis of a critical phenomenological method: (a) epoché, (b) deconstruction, (c) construction and (d) reflecting on phenomenologizing, and (e) reporting. Once again, we remind the readers that these steps are not as such consecutive procedures but enacted simultaneously and only for analytical purposes are they presented as distinct moments.

Epoché

Merleau-Ponty (1978) stated, "[T]he phenomenological world is not pure being, but the sense, which is revealed, where the paths of my various experiences intersect, and also where my own and other people intersect and engage each other like gears" (p. xx). Therefore, Scheler (1954) found that "the others" were presupposed in intentional acts. For example, he argued that most moral acts, such as "love, promise keeping and gratitude" (p. 229), contain a reference to other people, which demonstrates that "the essential character of human consciousness is such that the community is in some sense implicit in every individual" (p. 229).

Consequently, the Being of the lifeworld is given a priori through intersubjectivity as a "background" that makes it possible for the individual to posit "the reality of any possible object within it" (p. 236). Therefore, instead of putting the natural attitude out of play, as Husserl does in *Ideas*, critical phenomenology must examine its constitutive elements, specifically sedimented experiences of others and the community. Thus, in the words of Meagher (2021), we acknowledge that "there is a racist, colonialist natural attitude that saturates Euromodernity's overside: it is typical for each to uncritically take on a way of perceiving the world and its inhabitants" (p. 78).

In other words, the natural attitude is not natural at all, but generated from historical experiences of superiority and subjugation of non-Whites and women, and consequently, the "dominant interpretive approaches" in social research suffer from the limitations of this "hidden ideology" (p. 80). It is this colonial attitude we must attempt to bracket by rejecting the notion that our research methods are neutral and elevating Black- and female-embodied epistemological realities.

Deconstruction

We proceed by deconstructing the lifeworld to situations that actualize these embodied realities. In this connection, we are reminded of Sartre's (1992) axiom of the third ontological dimension of the body, where we apperceive our embodied selves from how others look at us in the situations we appear in (p. 461). Thus, Sartre stated, "[B]y situating me, the look defines me spatially and temporally" (as cited in McBride, 2020, p. 213). In this way, Simonsen and Koefod (2020) deploy a form of reduction that moves the researcher's gaze toward situations where the "I" encounters the "others" because "the designation of an "I" or a "we" requires a meeting with others" (p. 48).

Simonsen and Koefod (2020) proposed a three-dimensional research approach focusing on examining: (a) planned encounters, which are structured and managed situations, (b) encounters with authorities, and (c) everyday coincidental encounters in the public space (see p. 54). Simonsen and Koefod (2020) had a particular research agenda pertaining to the urban space of Copenhagen and therefore they did not consider other equally constitutive encounter-situations, such as (d) encounters with loved ones, (e) professional encounters in the workplace, or (f) online encounters on social media platforms.

Construction

Because we are aiming to produce nomothetic outcomes, a deconstruction of the constitutive elements of Being to mere situational encounters is not sufficient. Thus, Husserl (1977) challenges us to "inquire after what is typically universal, and even so extensively universal that we find it in every world experience" (p. 48). In this way, Burlew et al. (2019) cautioned against designing studies where the researchers compare Black populations with White populations because this approach suppresses the intergroup diversity and uniqueness of the Black population and often elevates the White sample population to "the gold standard against which the other group is evaluated" (p. 356).

Instead, Sousa (2017) proposed that a genetic analysis should involve "describing and interpreting meanings that have become sedimented during the course of personal development, at its different phases, during its interaction with the family and with social and cultural environments" (p. 110).

To this end, the previous deconstruction of the designation "I" or "we" into encounter-situations presents the researcher with an opportunity to engage in eidetic variation. In this manner, the researcher can begin to construct an ontology of the natural attitude and the life-world of women, Black people, and other marginalized populations by thematically describing the belief of being that are revealed throughout these encounters. In this way, Oksala (2022) suggested that politization and historization are essential for a critical phenomenological reduction, as they allow the "analyses to have a bite in the real world" (p. 8) by demonstrating all conceptions of race and gender are historically contingent.

Reflecting on Phenomenologizing

Scheler (1954, p. 216) posed a question still relevant for all stripes of social researchers: "By what right is a particular individual" entitled to postulate (a) the existence of a given community and (b) of some other given person? In this connection, Oksala (2022) argued that critical phenomenology should not only be directed at society but must also be critical of "its own methods, concepts, and limitations" (p. 10). For example, how did the researcher's analysis succeed in disrupting the colonial attitude? To what extent did the researcher reproduce said attitude?

The point of critical phenomenology is that there is no race- and gender-neutral point of view in social research. The eidetic analysis necessary to formulate a "theoretical truth" (Husserl, 1977, p. 48) about what it means to be woman, Black, etc., always takes place from the perspective of the researcher, and therefore Wertz (1985) warned that "the researcher's comprehension is challenged to find relevance anyway it can, and his choices are based in his specific ability to do so" (p. 167). Thus, the researcher carries the burden of proof pertaining to the credibility of the research outcome.

In this connection, Young (2004) raised the question of to what extent "being socially distant or dissimilar to the kinds of people under study affects both the richness or accuracy of the data being collected and the subsequent analysis that unfolds" (p. 187). Young (2004) provided an instructive example of how seemingly neutral questions were offensive to Black respondents. This does not mean that White researchers cannot conduct social research with Black subjects, but Simonsen and Koefod (2020) emphasized that the critical phenomenological method requires the researcher to reflect on differences (p. 10) and coexistence (p. 11), and the greater the distance is, the greater the divide to bridge is.

Reporting

In the phase of construction, we have come to understand Dasein of the Black person and the woman as a specific rule "in relation to what it encounters in the world" (Boss, 1982, p. 40), but de Beauvoir and Fanon did not engage in the problem of Being just to describe identities and posit on how they form. Their goal was also to create change by examining how this Being-for-the-others is construed and internalized so that the individual is empowered to change their understanding of self and others.

Fanon (2008) referred to this as a "desalination" (p. 206) of sedimented experiences that interrupt the ability of women, Black people, and other minorities to constitute themselves on their own terms. In this way, Heidegger (2010) likened consciousness to a silent call that summons Dasein "to one's own self" (p. 262), but this call is deceptive because "the call is heard in such a way that instead of being understood authentically, it is drawn by the they-self into a conversation with one's self in which one makes deals" (p. 264). Hence, Dasein can only "project itself upon the possibilities into which it is thrown" (p. 273), which means that the possibilities for self-constitution fall prey to "Das Man."

In practical terms, this issue relates to the question of equity in social research. Thus, researchers must ensure that their studies are not done on populations but with populations in such a way the outcomes will benefit the research populations, their communities, as well as the researcher, who ultimately gets to publish a paper or acquire a degree. For example, the researchers should make an effort at sharing the research with the populations and their communities and take the opportunity to process findings. The point is to use research to inter-rupt the deception of "Das Man" so that the subjects can come to see that there are possibilities for more authentic ways of being and iden-tify the barriers that prevent them from pursuing these possibilities.

In this connection, special care should be taken in choosing appro-priate terminologies, as words are vessels of sense. For example, many researchers use the standard race/ethnicity denominators as the U.S. government, but these include no variations in the category Black, irrespective of the diverse backgrounds of Black people living in the United States (Burlew et al., 2019, p. 357). Thus, Heidegger (1968) poetically warned that "this floundering in commonness is part of a high and dangerous game and gamble, in which, by the nature of lan-guage, we are the stakes" (p. 119).

Review of the Critical Phenomenological Research Literature

An instructive and recent example of applied feminist critical phe-nomenology is Welsh (2022), who explored how female self-care, body modification, and aesthetics develop socially and, therefore, how "to be a woman is to work on one's appearance" (p. 61). She explained how there are entirely different social expectations for how women should appear compared to men, which means that they apperceive their bodies as a work in progress. This in turn explains why anorexia and bulimia "occur predominantly among women" (p. 61).

Hence, the purpose of critical phenomenology is to disrupt the con-stitution of the female cultural body. This project should not be nar-rowly conceived as a struggle against male dominance since women themselves are equally complicit in reproducing and imposing bodily norms on themselves that are not necessarily a consequence of the male gaze but as much of a misguided notion that willing the body into a certain shape and look is a manifestation of individual freedom and agency of self. Under all circumstances, Welsh (2022) noted that men do not appear to equate agency with body control to the same degree as women, which indicates that more research is needed in this area for the sake of a more authentic physical and mental well-being of women.

Critical phenomenological research breaks with constructivism in the sense that the constitution of what is real is conceived from the first-person point of view. However, it is not uncommon to encounter published studies that aspire to critical phenomenology by combining the descriptive methods from IPA with the organizing lens of CRT. For example, Okoroji and Oka's (2021) study of how Black middle school adolescents experience discrimination. The problem with this approach is that CRT is defined by its anti-essentialism and posits that race is socially constructed, and their definitions are contingent on socioeconomic structures (see p. 456). In contrast, phenomenology is the study of essence, and to this end, the reduction is the signature method of phenomenology.

IPA does not make use of the reduction, which means that the findings of Okoroji and Oka (2021) remain idiographic rather than nomothetic. It is therefore an open question as to what we can learn about society by deploying a macro-theory such as CRT to illuminate highly contextual findings. In other words, only by confronting the perspective of theoretical generalization with generalizable findings are we able to construct new scientific knowledge. Therefore, Oksala (2022) insisted that the reduction is essential in phenomenological research, as it moves the findings from the concrete to the universal.

In contrast, Salamon's (2018b) critical phenomenological study examined how a person's gender that is different from the biological sex is constituted as an act of aggression by a person with a transphobic disposition, which, in the specific case of the student Latisha King, led to her murder (see p. 10). Salamon (2018b) observed that gender is experienced as a bodily enactment – for example, a way of walking – and that the transphobic perpetrator construed this as a form of sexual harassment (see p. 12). Thus, he saw himself as a victim defending against the invasiveness of the other's effeminate body language in his space.

Salamon (2018b) derived this interpretation from Merleau-Ponty's notion of embodiment, where the body signifies meaning, and she proceeded with projecting this incident onto a broader history of effeminate behavior and social consequence in the United States, and in this manner, emulated the historization that Oksala (2022) called for as part of the critical reduction. Consequently, the study transformed into a broader critique of White heteronormative society in terms of how gender is expected to be lived in accordance with sex. Here, Salamon (2018b) took up the latent theme of how the entire court proceeding, following the murder, was steeped in transphobic sensemaking from both teachers, witnesses, and lawyers, who conceived of King's body language as a risk and attention-seeking behavior (see p. 119) that had to be contained for her own good. These insights led Salamon (2018b) to reconnect with Sartre's ethical phenomenological perspective by raising the question, "What environment, what context within the school, would lead Brandon to the conclusion that he was "doing the right thing" in shooting Latisha King?" (p. 153).

Salamon (2018b) is however puzzled that Latisha's race never appeared as a theme of the court proceedings but was excluded since the pretrial concluded that race was not a motive and questioned the purpose of sequestering an essential dimension of the victim's Being. In this connection, Fanon's notion of the Black person being relegated to a zone of nonbeing comes to mind, and by entirely ignoring the question of race, the proceeding has made race a phenomenological problem in light of Sartre's (1992, p. 55) notion of nothingness. Without articulating it directly, the answer to Salamon's question is that negation and disruption of Latisha's self-constitution are the values we can assign to the social environment of the school and that the perpetrator chooses his selfness as a reflection of the values of this environment.

10 The Phenomenological Research Question

Heidegger (2010) explained that "questioning is a seeking," and "every seeking takes its lead beforehand from what is sought" (p. 4). By this, he meant that the question is a clearing that allows the researcher to see the phenomenon in a certain way, and therefore the research question is already committed to a certain theoretical frame of reference. In this connection, Heidegger identified three moments of the questioning, which are better expressed in German than in English: The "Gefragtes," "Befragtes," and "Erfragtes" (p. 4). "Das Gefragtes" refers to the topic of interest, for example, the situation we are inquiring about. "Das Befragtes" refers to our method of questioning that creates a particular clearing for the phenomenon and allows us to acquire a certain type of knowledge, which is "Das Erfragtes." In other words, the phenomenological research question should take its lead from the type of knowledge we already know we are seeking. Thus, Merleau-Ponty (Edie, 2000, p. 58) reminded us that "it is very evident that induction will remain blind if we do not know in some other way, and indeed from inside consciousness itself, what this induction is dealing with" (Edie, 2000, p. 58).

In the previous chapters, we have clarified that the schism in phenomenology can be traced back to the dichotomy between the two concepts in Descartes's maxim: *Cogito ergo sum* (I think therefore I am). Therefore, the problem of constitution can either be elucidated from the perspective of consciousness and mind or from Dasein and comportment depending on whether we find essence or existence to be aprioric. Therefore, a theoretical sound research question already presupposes either of the two perspectives.

DOI: 10.4324/9781003270058-10

Phenomenological Psychology

The problem phenomenological psychology is preoccupied with is that in the natural attitude, we are focused on appearances of things and situations without noticing that these appearances are constituted by a "psychical act of experience" (Kockelmans, 1987, p. 13). For example, many of Husserl's thought experiments pertain to static examinations of perceptual experiences of specific objects such as a piece of white paper, a table, a house, etc., where he attempts to work out how the objectifying structures of subjectivity shape the experience.

In this way, the Dutch and later the Duquesne schools of phenomenological psychology applied Husserl's theories and methods for the purpose of clarifying the essential meaning of psychological concepts the modern sciences use to describe and measure the lifeworld of human beings (Kockelmans, 1987, p. 6). For example, Wertz's (1985) research question "what is criminal victimization?" (p. 158) speaks to the field of social psychology as the study attempted to clarify the meaning of this concept by researching a range of experiences, where subjects have been submitted to everything from burglaries to attempted rape. On an entirely different topic, Wertz and Greenhut (1985) set out to investigate *what buying is* by asking the following research questions: What is "the meaning, purpose and structure of buying, and how the value of a purchase is constituted"? (p. 566).

In both cases, the phenomenological method is applied to isolate the invariant structures (Steinbock, 1998, p. 129) of these experiences and thereby clarify the ontology behind the concepts that serve to objectify them as types of experiences. From time to time, the eidetic method uncovers that the salient experiences underpinning these concepts are either too diverse to be housed under one concept or that the concept is not reflective of the underlying experiences. In such cases, the analysis may give rise to the formation of new concepts, revisions, or retirement of existing concepts. For example, the study of intense combat experiences has given rise to concepts such as soldier's heart, shells shock, and Vietnam syndrome, which were ultimately retired in favor of "a diagnosis and phenomenological description of PTSD" (Crocq & Crocq, 2000, p. 53).

Genetic Phenomenology

Genetic phenomenology is preoccupied with the domains of time-consciousness and apperception, and according to Ashworth (2016), this translates into a broad type of research question such as "what is it like to experience something like this?" The rather insignificant words "what is it like" connect with phenomenological psychology not only in terms of what something feels like but also point to the constitution of the lifeworld. It refers to the "aboutness" of situations where subjects actualize their experience as types of experiences (i.e., judgments). The theoretical assumption is that judgments are temporal phenomena and must be analyzed accordingly. For example, Hvidt (2017) described what the transformative experience of a "cancer journey" is like.

Researching Dasein

On the other side of the cogito ergo sum equation, Heidegger (2010) argued that "to describe the world phenomenologically means to show and conceptually and categorically determine the Being of beings present in the world" (p. 63). Consequently, our research question in existential phenomenology always pertains to Being in its abstract form. However, the previous elaborations demonstrated that Being must be elucidated through an interrogation of Dasein because Dasein unites the ontic with the ontological. While Heidegger's ontological phenomenology takes aim at Being from an interpretation of what Dasein cares about, and Sartre's philosophy looks at how free will constituted Being as a value, then Ricoeur's hermeneutical phenomenology essentially wants to know who Beings are. We can call this the: W*hat*, *how*, and *who* of Dasein analysis.

For example, Darbyshire and Oerther (2021) used Heidegger's Dasein theory to elucidate what being a parent in challenging times means. Heidegger (2002) argued that challenges are the framework that "places man and Being face to face" (p. 35) and where the force of this challenge delivers the human being to the ownership of Being (p. 36). Consequently, this study did not come to an answer by investigating judgment, meaning making, or roles. Instead, the researchers focused on the way parents become attuned to their environment in new ways as things they did not care about before suddenly came into the forefront. In this manner, the investigation considers being a parent as a range of possibilities for being.

The applied literature is not overflowing with examples of research framed by Dasein. However, we are reminded that when Dasein speaks, it is not the authentic individual we hear; rather, it is Das Man, "the nobody whom the everyday Dasein has always surrendered itself" (Heidegger, 2010, p. 124). Dasein is therefore not a private psychological affair but publicness, and with the emergence of social media, it is possible that a new realm of Dasein analysis is emerging. Social media studies almost never take their starting point in the voice of a known subject but instead study the voice of the community, which can be understood as the digital equivalent of Das Man. For example, Lagerkvist's (2017) study of "digital thrownness" alluded to Heidegger's notion of Dasein being thrown into an already existing world and attempted to illuminate the question "what does it mean to be a human being in the digital age?" (p. 97) and "what does being there signify in a digital culture?" (p. 105).

Critical Phenomenology

Drawing on the feminist tradition of Simone de Beauvoir, Oksala (2006) suggested that research should question "how gendered experiences are constituted and how their constitution is tied not only to embodiment, but also to the normative cultural practices and structures of meaning" (p. 240). In this manner, we would be articulating research questions that not only focus on elucidating first-person experiences but also the historicity of gender in general.

For example, de Beauvior (2015) presented a freedom-oriented research agenda for feminist phenomenology with the following questions: How can a female accomplish herself? "What paths are open to her? Which ones lead to dead ends? How can she find independence within dependence? What circumstances limit women's freedom and can she overcome them?" (p. 24). Ultimately, de Beauvoir raised the question "Do women exist?" (Bergoffen, 2020, p. 122) in a challenge to how the feminine has been conceptualized by the male gaze since biblical times.

Salamon (2018a) argued that critical phenomenology should focus on examining oppression by asking questions beginning with "in what way and by what right?" (p. 13). More specifically, Maegher (2021) proposed that critical phenomenologists can challenge colonization by asking questions such as "How do the words of this agent of coloniality maintain and conceal the colonial difference?," and "How can an agent at once maintain and conceal the colonial difference?" (p. 82).

In contrast, Burlew et al. (2019) suggested that researchers should focus on "the unique characteristics of their target group" (p. 355) and refrain from formulating deficiency research questions and instead focus on "strength-based approaches" (p. 355), for example, studying successful Black populations. In this connection, the editors of the journal *Child & Youth Services* (Gharabaghi and Anderson-Nathe, 2017) stated, "In reviewing the research literature that comes across our desks through this journal, and the literature we see appear in other journals, we lament just how little we know about what young people living in precarious circumstances do well" (p. 178).

The point is to develop research that refocuses from critically exposing oppression to generating knowledge that can assist historically oppressed populations in overcoming structural barriers. Hence, it all begins with asking the necessary questions, and as Heidegger stated, the question is a clearing made by us that allows the phenomenon to show itself in a certain way.

11 The Phenomenological Interview

It is taken for granted that the primary method for gathering data in a phenomenological study is the interview, and the interview transcript is the de facto data set most researchers process by this or that analytical or interpretative move. Some researchers rely on various software with the ability to categorize textual data. This produces a range of content thematic categories, and some researchers will proceed with the assumption that they have somehow thematized the experience. The problem with this is that researchers fail to properly consider "the epistemological status" of the interview (Schutz, 1972, p. xxii). In other words, the content of the interview does not directly represent the experience; rather, it is a range of answers to questions that the researchers have posed and therefore what Paley (2014) calls an "artefact of being interviewed." In this manner, we can say that the interview situation causes the researcher to become a theme in the phenomenological investigation and because it is futile to prevent this from happening, we can instead try to control how it happens through a careful conceptualization of experience, subject, and research question.

Thus, the researcher must try to frame the interview within the phenomenological theories that inform the domain that they are trying to study. The point is that phenomenology is not merely a research method like generic qualitative research, but ultimately a methodology that is designed to tease out the genesis of constitution, and therefore our theoretical understanding of the relevant domains must inform both the research questions and ensure that the interview questions are aligned accordingly.

Thus, Chapter 3 demonstrated that when researchers conceive the human subject in terms of Dasein, the notion of subjectivity must be bracketed and replaced by a "they-self." For most researchers, it is tremendously difficult to bracket a culture of psychologization because

DOI: 10.4324/9781003270058-11

psychologism is a characteristic of the natural attitude. Therefore, studies that invoke Dasein and interpretation often end up haunted by psychology. Thus, the theoretical position that our subjects' selfhood, ideas, beliefs, and understandings ultimately belong to Das Man and that Dasein, therefore, is publicness is alien and at the same time frightening as the rejection of ego ultimately inflicts some existential pain on the researchers themselves.

Paley (2014) suggested that researchers basing their studies on Heidegger should abandon the concept of lived experience altogether. In this connection, Larsen and Adu (2021) explained that in ontological phenomenology, Dasein does not constitute the world through perceptions, but instead comes to an understanding of its meaning through "circumspection" (p. 22), which is the practical engagement with whatever is ready-to-hand. Thus, Being is constituted through acts of care and not Erlebnis, but many phenomenological researchers confound those terms and therefore also confuse understanding with perception.

The consequence of theoretically conceptualizing the subject as either ego or a "they-self" and aligning experiencing as apperception and care, respectively, is that the researchers need to ask different interview questions. For example, if the subject's intentionality is care, then we need to direct the interview toward situations where the subject is doing exactly that (i.e., taking care of the project of living life in-order-to and for-the-sake of something). In contrast, if the subject's intentionality is mental, we would be more interested in their thoughts, hereunder how their experiencing actualizes in judgments and the psychological genesis of this act.

Under all circumstances, most applied research begins with a situation that is directly experienced by the subjects, which is what we would call the ontic phenomenon. Hence, we are not interested in what the subjects think about certain ideas or concepts. The phenomenon is not an ideal object, but initially a phenomenal experience of a concrete situation (Englander & Morley, 2021).

Heidegger (2002) argued that challenging situations are the framework that "places man and Being face to face" (p. 35) and where the force of this challenge delivers the human being to the ownership of Being (p. 36). Heidegger (2002) referred to this moment as "the event of appropriation" (p. 36). Therefore, the interview questions must be directed at these situations, asking what the individual "had to find, and how it had to encounter itself, or how it bears within itself a rule of individual character traits that are recognizable" (Steinbock, 1998, p. 14).

In this connection, we can distinguish phenomenological psychology and hermeneutic phenomenology by orienting our interview questions toward either judgment or care. If we conceive of the actualized experience in terms of a judgment, we would then be asking questions as to how our subjects conceive of their situations. In contrast, if the researchers conceive the experience as care, we will ask about their actions and how they handled things.

The point is to use the interview questions to acquire relevant data for the domain we are investigating and ensure that the data are useful for the specific methodology belonging to that domain. However, Petitmengin (2006) acknowledged that phenomenological psychological researchers are confronted with the problem that instead of describing the experience, subjects describe a "representation of this experience" (p. 235) and convey a general judgment about the situation they found themselves in. This judgment is not the experience, but rather the experiences actualized in a judgment, and, to acquire data about the subjective act generating this judgment, he proposed that the researchers ask "how" questions. The purpose is to deflect the subject's attention from the description of the whatness of the situation and refocus on how the situation appears to be meaningful. To this end, it is equally important to focus the interview on singular situations to prevent the discourse from wandering into abstractions and conversations about situations in general (p. 242).

Further, Petitmengin (2006) explained that researchers can minimize the risk of becoming a theme in their own studies by asking their subjects "content-empty" (p. 248) interview questions. By this she means questions that do not impose the researchers' presuppositions of what the subjects' experiences are like, but instead direct their attention to the various temporal phases of their experiences, i.e., from beginning to end.

In addition, Bevan (2014) suggested that the interviewer can incorporate elements of imaginative variation by asking questions about similar but still hypothetical situations. The purpose would be to understand if the act of judging is contingent on the particular situation or whether it would be the same in other but similar situations. For example, "Would you have reacted differently if the person was younger? Would you have acted differently if it were a woman?" (Larsen & Adu, 2021, p. 219).

Sousa (2017) presented a range of cases from which it is possible to glean examples of phenomenological psychological questions. For example, "How so?" (p. 186) is a response question to a subject's judgment about what a situation is and aims to deconstruct how the subject came to this conclusion. Further, Sousa articulated more mundane questions that mostly orbited around the constitutive how. For example, "How do you feel when … ?" (p. 187), and "How was it always this way?" (p. 187). Followed up by, "What do you mean with … ?" (p. 187), "How did it happen for you…?" (p. 188) "What's it like for you?" (p. 198), and "How do you understand this?" (p. 199).

Petitmengin (2006) also emphasized that the interviewer may ascertain the validity of the disclosures from the subject's "quality of contact with the experience" (p. 258) from body language. In this way, we are reminded of Merleau-Ponty's (1978, p. 185) insight that gestures are not symbolic of experience but are the experience itself, and gesticulations are therefore to be understood as a moment where the subject is in direct contact with the experience (Petitmengin, 2006, p. 257). Consequently, this type of observational data is more trustworthy than words, because our theoretical understanding of the subject and the act of experience informs us that not only is the subject embedded in the situation, but the situation is also embodied in the subject (Høffding & Martiny, 2016).

Turning to Dasein, the interview questions will acquire a different flavor, as we are trying to gain data pertaining to comportemental behavior we call care. Høffding and Martiny (2016) recommended leveraging the methodology introduced by Vermersch' in his 1994 book *Explication Interview (EI)*. This work has however not been available in English until 2017 and then in a somewhat awkward translation. Nevertheless, the point of EI is to facilitate the epoché already at the interview stage (p. 552), and in this connection, Vermersch (2017, p. 63) suggested that we avoid questions that induce conceptualization. For example, Graf and Fleischhacker's (2020) discourse analysis of coaching situations demonstrated how an overtly conceptualized language diverted from the actual professional praxis of their clients and instead reproduced the theoretical perspectives of the coaches.

Further, Vermersch (2017) suggested being true to avoid "why" questions that motivate a causality-based explication of the experience, which is prohibited in phenomenology (p. 105). Finally, he suggested that the interviewer allows the subjects to guide the interview back to what is relevant by asking questions such as, "Choose a moment that is important to you or choose a moment that interests you or the moment that comes to mind first" (p.102). Finally, Vermersch (2017, p. 106) proposed the following interview questions, focusing on actions:

The beginning:
"How did you start?"
"What did you do first?"
"What was the starting point of your action?"
"What happened first?"
"How did you identify the problem that needed to be resolved?"

The sequence of actions:
"What did you do next?"
"And then what did you do?"
"And just after that, what did you take into account?" –

The end of the action:
"What happened at the end?"
"How did you finish?"
"What did you do last?"
"How did you know it was finished?"
"How did you know there was nothing left to do?"

(p. 106)

From these examples, we can see that none of the questions introduce a concept or an ideal object or imply any theoretical constructs. Nor do these questions imply any form of causality in the experience nor are they inducing a psychologization of the experience. The focus is on action and the project the individual was engaged in.

From the perspective of critical phenomenology, these types of interview questions are conceived as sanitized and equated with a White and masculine research approach, which lacks the crucial element of rapport based on shared gender (Oakley, 2016) and race. Hereunder,

empowerment of participants; hearing often silenced voices; minimising the power hierarchy between researcher and participant; encouraging the participant to lead research; equal sharing of opinions, thoughts, and ideas to minimise the exploitation of the participant (by taking their data, while giving nothing in return).

(Thwaites, 2017)

In the context of critical phenomenological research, we cannot utilize the "content-empty" questioning style that Petitmengin (2006) suggested. The interview questions must acknowledge the embodied reality of women, Black people, and other minorities as factual, as well as the historical conditions of oppression and marginalization. To a certain degree, the interviewer takes the side of the subjects, which is a delicate balance, as the interviewer must also remain critical when colonial and oppressive themes are being reproduced. The point is that the subjects must get something out of this procedure as well.

Further, we cannot hope to immediately achieve a genuine level of rapport between interviewers and subjects who are too different culturally, racially, sexually, and gender-wise. In this connection, Lamont's (2004) reflections on her experiences interviewing subjects across these divides are instructive. One of her many points was that subjects vastly different from her made her cultural background and her sex a salient theme in the interview. In other cases, subjects for whom Princeton University means nothing would assume that she might work for the government and would bring their visas to the interview.

12 Decision Tree

The previous chapters have provided insights into the different phenomenological schools and how they conceptualize and study the question of constitution. Thus, alignment between theory and method provides the research outcomes some credibility. However, the choice between the various domains and methodologies always begins with an identified gap in the literature about an ongoing problem. The literature offers up clues in the form of various authors' suggestions for future studies. These suggestions often express the need for investigating experiences, understandings, beliefs, identities, and even ethics and because phenomenology presupposes that the life world is constituted and not constructed, the approach tends to be first-person point of view research with all the bells and whistles described in the previous chapters.

The challenge can be to look beyond the terminology that researchers often use somewhat callously. For example, the notion of lived experience and perception. As the previous elaboration demonstrated, the meanings of these terms in the foundational literature are often something entirely different from how they are presented in the secondary literature, which is what most of us actually read. In fact, perception is a lived experience. We should therefore not put much stock into the notion of lived experience and instead simply understand that some form of direct experience should be the source of our data gathering. In terms of perception, we should conceive this as a call to study how subjectivity phenomenologically shapes the world into somebody's life world. It is again important to note that in phenomenology, perception is not "an act of deliberate taking up a position; it is the background from which all acts stand out" (Merleau-Ponty, 1978, p. xi). In other words, perceptions are not opinions.

DOI: 10.4324/9781003270058-12

In a similar fashion, suggestions for future studies that pertain to being, what it means to be, or how concepts are understood generally or within a particular profession would fall under existential phenomenology. For example, there is a distinction between studying the psychological problem of what it is like to live through cancer and what it means to be a cancer survivor, not to speak of the ontological question of what surviving actually means in this context.

In contrast, we have suggestions for research that are more action oriented, presuppose certain injustices, and imply that the researcher needs to reveal oppressive or colonial dimensions of our lifeworld. These suggestions should be answered by critical phenomenology if they are truly focused on the problem of selfhood, empowerment, and agency. In other words, phenomenology should remain focused on the problem of constitution and, in this case, the questions of what it means to be woman, Black, disabled, gay, transgender, etc., are within the realm of critical phenomenology.

The following two illustrations represent a "family tree" and a domain overview (Figures 12.1 and 12.2). These illustrations essentially summarize the previous chapters and provide a decision-making framework when designing a phenomenological study in terms of theories, the foundational authors one should consult, and the appropriate methods aligned with each domain. It may be a good idea to begin the research project by contrasting the identified research gap with the overview in figure two and consider which of the listed domains or

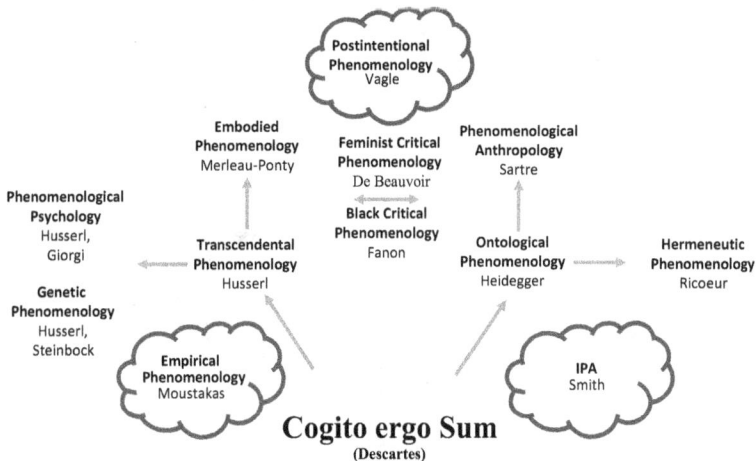

Figure 12.1 The phenomenological family tree.

Phenomenological domains:	School:	The research subject:	Methods:	Authors:
Givenness and essence	Transcendental phenomenology	Transcendental ego	Epoché and reduction	Husserl
Perception and world	Embodied phenomenology	Embodied ego	Epoché and reduction	Merleau-Ponty
Apperception and lifeworld	Phenomenological psychology	Psychological ego	Psychological epoche and reduction	Husserl/Giorgi
Judgments and Lifeworld	Genetic phenomenology	Psychological ego	Ontological reduction (Abbau)	Husserl/Steinbock
Care and Being	Ontological phenomenology	"They-self"/Dasein	Dasein analysis	Heidegger
Free will and Being-for-itself	Phenomenological anthropology	Self	*Psychanalyse Existentielle*	*Sartre*
Emplotment and identity	Hermeneutic phenomenology	Narrative self	Double Hermeneutics: Distanciation	Ricoeur
Being-for-the-other	Feminist critical phenomenology	Woman	Critical method	De Beauvoir
Non-Being and Blackness	Black critical phenomenology	Black double consciousness	Critical method	Fanon/Dubois

Figure 12.2 The phenomenological domains.

conceptualizations of the research subject best capture the essential meaning of the identified research gap. Then subsequently, consult the relevant chapters in this book for further insights into theory and methods. The previous chapters contain extensive references to the foundational literature, which may assist the reader in further exploring phenomenology.

Future Research

It should be noted that the book has omitted the emerging literature on queer phenomenology. Hereunder Ahmed's (2006) book carrying this title explores what it means for "sexuality to orientated" (p. 1). Ahmed pursues two strategies: (1) "[q]ueering phenomenology" (p. 5), where she examines queer moments in the phenomenological literature for example pertaining to Merleau-Ponty's theories of embodiment, and (2) "moving queer theory toward phenomenology" (p. 5). However, Ahmed considers her work more a starting point and refrains from prescribing "[w]hat forms queer phenomenology should take" (p. 5). Therefore, this author calls for further development of this domain for inclusion in a future edition of this book.

On a similar note, this author would like to see a future edition of this book include a phenomenological perspective on disability or vice versa. In this connection, Abrams (2016) examines Heidegger's concept of the ontological difference between beings and Being through the lens of disability. However, a further examination of visible and invisible disabilities from a phenomenological perspective is required. In this connection, the ontological difference that Abrams examines should be understood more in terms of the existential comportment of both the persons with disabilities toward what is ready-to-hand and in terms of the comportment of those without disabilities toward the disabled.

Finally, phenomenology must step up to the challenges of virtual reality and the emerging metaverse and consider the phenomenon of double-constitution, where on one hand the subject comports toward a new dimension of reality and in this manner makes it meaningful, but on the other hand, the metaverse is a reality by design constituted by intent and with intentions. Thus, from the perspective of the metaverse, human subjects are beings-for-it. It is an ontological structure, a happening Dasein, where we are not the ready-to-hand phenomena.

References

Abrams, T. (2016). *Heidegger and the politics of disablement*. Palgrave Pivot.

Ahmed, S. (2006). *Queer phenomenology: Orientations, objects, others*. Duke University Press.

Alcoff, L. M. (1999). Towards a phenomenology of racial embodiment. *Radical Philosophy*, *495*, 15–26.

Alves, P. M. (2021). Genesis. In D. De Santis, B. C. Hopkins, & C. Majolino (Eds.), The *Routledge handbook of phenomenology and phenomenological philosophy* (pp. 207–220). Routledge.

Arp, K. (2005). The joys of disclosure: Simone de Beauvoir and the phenomenological tradition. In A. Tymieniecka (Ed.), *Logos of phenomenology and phenomenology of the Logos. Book one* (pp. 393–406). Springer.

Ashworth, P. D. (2009). William James's "psychologist's fallacy" and contemporary human science research. *International Journal of Qualitative Studies on Health and Well-being*, *4*(4), 195–206. https://doi.org/10.3109/17482620903223036

Ashworth, P. D. (2016). The lifeworld-enriching qualitative evidence. *Qualitative Research in Psychology*, *13*(1), 20–32. https://doi.org/10.1080/14780887.2015.1076917

Ashworth, P. D. (2017). Interiority, exteriority and the realm of intentionality. *Journal of Phenomenological Psychology*, *48*(1), 39–62. https://doi.org/10.1163/15691624-12341321

Asthana, S. (2017). Youth, self, other: A study of Ibdaa's digital media practices in the West Bank, Palestine. *International Journal of Cultural Studies*, *20*(1), 100–117. https://doi.org/10.1177/1367877915600546

Barber, M. D. (2015). Apperception, the influence of culture and interracial humor. In M. J. Rozbicki (Ed.), *Perspectives on interculturality. The construction of meaning in relationship of difference* (pp. 27–38). Palgrave Macmillan.

Bas, L., & Van Manen, M. (2002). Phenomenological anthropology in the Netherlands and Flanders. In T. Tymieniecka (Ed.), *Phenomenology worldwide* (pp. 274–286). Kluwer Press.

Belt, J. (2021). Eidetic variation: A self-correcting and integrative account. *Axiomathes* https://doi.org/10.1007/s10516-021-09611-1

Bergoffen, D. (2018). Simone de Beauvoir. Philosopher, author, feminist. In D. Zahavi (Ed.), *The Oxford handbook of the history of phenomenology* (pp. 320–339). Oxford University Press.

Bergoffen, D. (2020). The eternal feminine. In G. Weiss, A. V. Murphy, & G. Salamon (Eds.), *50 concepts for a critical phenomenology* (pp. 121–126). Northwestern University Press.

Bevan, M. T. (2014). A method of phenomenological interviewing. *Qualitative Health Research, 24*(1), 136–144. https://doi.org/10.1177/1049732313519710

Bolton, D., & Gillet, G. (2019). *Biopsychosocial model of health and disease. New philosophical and scientific developments.* Palgrave Macmillan. https://doi.org/10.1007/978-3-030-11899-0

Boss M. (1982). *Psychoanalysis and daseinanalysis.* Dacapo Press.

Boss, M. (2000). Recent considerations in daseinsanalysis. *The Humanistic Psychologist, 28*(1–3), 210–230. https://doi.org/10.1080/08873267.2000.9976992

Bower, M. E. M. (2020). Finding a way into genetic phenomenology. In I. Apostolescu (Ed.), *The subject(s) of phenomenology. Contributions to phenomenology, 108* (pp. 185–200) Springer Cham. https://doi.org/10.1007/978-3-030-29357-4_10

Burlew, A. K., Peteet, B. J., McCuistian, C., & Miller-Roenigk, B. D. (2019). Best practices for researching diverse groups. *American Journal of Orthopsychiatry, 89*(3), 354–368. https://doi.org/10.1037/ort0000350

Butler, J. L. (2016). Rediscovering Husserl: Perspectives on the epoché and the reductions. *The Qualitative Report, 21*(11), 2033–2043. https://doi.org/10.46743/2160-3715/2016.2327

Chernavin, G. I. (2016). The process of sense-formation and fixed sense-structures: Key intuitions in the phenomenology of Edmund Husserl. *Russian Studies in Philosophy, 54*(1), 48–61.

Churchill. S. D. (2022). *Existential phenomenological research.* American Psychological Association.

Collins, D. E. (2020a). American culture sees Blackness as the damage it did to us, not the joy we take in ourselves. https://www.nbcnews.com/think/opinion/american-culture-sees-blackness-damage-it-did-us-not-joy-ncna1235703

Collins, P. H. (2020b). Controlling images. In G. Weiss, A. V. Murphy, & G. Salamon (Eds.), *50 concepts for a critical phenomenology* (pp. 77–82). Northwestern University Press.

Craig, E. (2019). The history of Daseinanalysis. In E. V. Duerzen, E. Craig, A. L. Kirk, J. Schneider, D. Tantam, & S. D. Plock (Eds.), *The Wiley world handbook of existential therapy* (pp. 33–54). John Wiley & Sons Ltd.

Creswell, J. W. (2007). *Qualitative inquiry & research design: Choosing among five approaches.* SAGE.

Crocq, M. A., & Crocq, L. (2000). From shell shock and war neurosis to post-traumatic stress disorder: A history of psychotraumatology. *Dialogues in Clinical Neuroscience, 2*(1), 47–55. https://doi.org/10.31887/DCNS.2000.2.1/macrocq

Darbyshire, P., & Oerther, S. (2021). Heidegger and parenthood: A theoretical and methodological shift from instrumental to ontological understanding. *Journal of Child Health Care, 25*(4), 523–533. https://doi.org/10.1177/1367493520965836

Darian, P. (2015). *Sartre and no child left behind: An existential psychoanalytic anthropology of urban schooling.* Lexington Books.

Davidson, S. (2016). Intersectional hermeneutics. In S. Davidson & M. A. Vallée (Eds.), *Hermeneutics and phenomenology in Paul Ricoeur: Between text and phenomenon* (pp. 159–174). Springer International Publishing.

Davies, D. H. (2020). The phenomenological method. In G. Weiss, A. V. Murphy, & G. Salamon (Eds.), *50 concepts for a critical phenomenology* (pp. 3–9). Northwestern University Press.

de Beauvior, S. (2015). *The second sex.* Vintage Books.

de Faria Blanc, M. (2005). The phenomenology and hermeneutics of traditions. In A. T. Tymieniecka (Ed.), *Logos of phenomenology and phenomenology of the logos. Book one* (pp. 37–48). Analecta Husserliana, vol 88. Springer, Dordrecht. https://doi.org/10.1007/1-4020-3680-9_2

DeRobertis, E. M., & Bland, A. M. (2020). From personal threat to cross-cultural learning: An eidetic investigation. *Journal of Phenomenological Psychology, 51*, 1–15.

Desai, M. U. (2022). Psychology, the psychological, and critical praxis: A phenomenologists reads Frantz Fanon. In L. Laubscher, D. Hook, & M. U. Desai (Eds.), *Fanon, phenomenology, and psychology* (pp. 73–88). Routledge.

Descartes, R. (1911). *Meditations on first philosophy.* Cambridge University Press.

Dreyfus, H. L. (1995). *Being-in-the-world: A complimentary on Heidegger's being and time, division 1.* The MIT Press.

Drummond, J. J. (2003). The structure of intentionality. In D. Welton (Ed.), *The new Husserl. A critical readers* (pp. 65–92). Indiana University Press.

Drummond, J. J. (2007). *Historical dictionary of Husserl's philosophy.* The Scarecrow Press, Inc.

Drummond, J. J. (2021). Ethics. In D. De Santis, B. C. Hopkins, & C. Majolino (Eds.), *The Routledge handbook of phenomenology and phenomenological philosophy* (pp. 207–220). Routledge.

Du Bois, W. E. B. (1994). *The souls of black folk.* Gramercy Books

Dwyer, D. J. (2007). Husserl's appropriation of the psychological concepts of apperception and attention. *Husserl Studies, 23*, 83–118. https://doi.org/10.1007/s10743-007-9020-4

Eagly, A. H., & Chaiken, S. (1993). *The psychology of attitudes.* Harcourt Brace Jovanovich College Publishers.

Eatough, V., & Smith, J. A. (2017). Interpretative phenomenological analysis. In C. Willig & W. Stainton-Rogers (Eds.), *The SAGE handbook of qualitative research in psychology* (pp. 193–209). Sage Publications.

Edie, J. M. (2000). *The primacy of perception.* Northwestern University Press.

Eidelson, R., & Eidelson, J. (2003). Dangerous ideas: Five beliefs that propel groups toward conflict. *The American Psychologist, 58*, 182–192. https://doi.org/10.1037/0003-066X.58.3.182

Englander, M., & Morley, J. (2021). Phenomenological psychology and qualitative research. *Phenomenology and the Cognitive Sciences.* https://doi.
org/10.1007/s11097-021-09781-8

Fanon, F. (2008). *Black skin white masks.* Grove Press.

Fink, Eugen (1995). *Sixth Cartesian meditation: The idea of a transcendental
theory of method.* Indiana University Press.

Fréchette, G. (2017). Brentano on time-consciousness. In U. Kriegel (Ed.), *Routledge
handbook of Franz Brentano and the Brentano school* (pp. 75–86). Routledge.

Fredholm, A., Manninen, K., Hjelmqvist, H., & Silén, C. (2019). Authenticity
made visible in medical students' experiences of feeling like a doctor.
International Journal of Medical Education, 10(1), 113–121. https://doi.
org/10.5116/ijme.5cf7.d60c

Gantt, E. E., & Williams, R. N. (2020). Methodological naturalism, satura-
tion, and Psychology's failure to save the phenomena. *Journal for the Theory
of Social Behaviour, 50*(1), 84–102.

Geniusas, S. (2020). Husserl's concepts of apperception and weltapperzeption.
In K. Novotny & C. Nielsen (Eds.), *Die Welt und das Reale / The world and
the real / Le monde et le reel.* Traugott Bautz (Libri Nigri, 78).

Gharabaghi, K., & Anderson-Nathe, B. (Eds.). (2017). Strength-based research
in a deficits-oriented context, *Child & Youth Services, 38*(3), 177–179.
https://doi.org/10.1080/0145935X.2017.1361661

Giorgi, A. (Ed.). (1985). *Phenomenology and psychological research.* Duquesne
University Press.

Giorgi, A. (2004). A way to overcome the methodological vicissitudes involved
in researching subjectivity. *Journal of Phenomenological Psychology, 35*(1),
1–25. https://doi.org/10.1163/1569162042321107

Giorgi, A. (2006). Concerning variations in the application of the phenomenological method. *The Humanistic Psychologist, 34*(4), 305–319. https://doi.
org/10.1207/s15473333thp3404_2

Giorgi, A. (2009). *The descriptive phenomenological method in psychology. A
modified Husserlian approach.* Duquesne University Press.

Giorgi, A. (2010). Phenomenology and the practice of science. *Journal of the
Society for Existential Analysis, 21*(1), 3–23.

Giorgi, A. (2011). IPA science: A response to Jonathan Smith. *Journal of Phenomenological Psychology, 42*(2), 195–216. https://doi.org/10.1163/156916211X599762

Giorgi, A. (2019). *Psychology as a human science: A phenomenologically based
approach.* University Professors Press.

Graf, E. M., & Fleischhacker, M. (2020). "Wenn ich es nicht schaffe, liegt es an
meiner Person und nicht an meiner Leistung" – Die Individualisierung struk-
tureller Probleme im Coaching weiblicher Führungskräfte. Genderlinguistische
und gendertheoretische Erkenntnisse für die Praxis. *Coaching Theorie &
Praxis.* https://doi.org/10.1365/s40896-020-00034-0

Guenther, L. (2020). Critical phenomenology. In G. Weiss, A. V. Murphy, & G.
Salamon (Eds.), *50 concepts for a critical phenomenology* (pp. 11–16).
Northwestern University Press.

Guignon, C. B. (1983). *Heidegger and the problem of knowledge.* Hackett.

Hanna, R. (2014) Husserl's crisis and our crisis. *International Journal of Philosophical Studies, 22*(5), 752–770. https://doi.org/10.1080/09672559.2014.977540

Hart, J. G. (2020). *Hedwig Conrad-Martius' ontological phenomenology.* Springer.

Heidegger, M. (1968). *What is called thinking?* Harper & Row.

Heidegger, M. (1977). *Basic writings.* Harper & Row.

Heidegger, M. (1988). *The basic problems of phenomenology.* Indiana University Press.

Heidegger, M. (2001a). *The concept of time.* Blackwell.

Heidegger, M. (2001b). *Poetry, language and thought.* Harper Perennial.

Heidegger, M. (2002). *Identity and difference.* The University of Chicago Press.

Heidegger, M. (2010). *Being and time.* University of New York Press.

Heidegger, M. (2014). *Introduction to metaphysics.* Yale University Press.

Heidegger, M., & Boss, M. (2001). *Zollikon seminars: Protocols, conversations, letters.* Northwestern University Press.

Heisenberg, W. (2007). *Physics and philosophy. The revolution in modern science.* HarperCollins.

Høffding, S., & Martiny, K. (2016). Framing a phenomenological interview: What, why and how. *Phenomenology and the Cognitive Sciences, 15,* 539–564. http://dx.doi.org/10.1007/s11097-015-9433-z

Husserl. E. (1960). *Cartesian meditations.* Springer-Science.

Husserl, E. (1970). *The crisis of European sciences and transcendental phenomenology: An introduction to phenomenological philosophy.* Northwestern University Press.

Husserl, E. (1973a). *The idea of phenomenology.* Martinius Nijhoff.

Husserl, E. (1973b). *Experience and judgment.* Northwestern University Press.

Husserl, E. (1977). *Phenomenological psychology.* Martinius Niijhoff.

Husserl, E. (2001a). *The shorter logical investigations.* Routledge.

Husserl, E. (2001b). *Analyses concerning passive and active synthesis. Lectures on transcendental logic.* Kluwer Academic Publishers.

Husserl, E. (2012). Das Konstitutionsproblem und der Sinn der konstitutiven Betrachtung bei Edmund Husserl (1957/63). In R. Fieguth, G. Küng, & W. Galewicz (Eds.), *Band 5 Schriften zur Phänomenologie Edmund Husserls* (pp. 237–267). De Gruyter. https://doi.org/10.1515/9783110916416.237

Husserl, E. (2017). Ideas: *General introduction to pure phenomenology.* Unwin Brothers Ltd.

Husserl, E. (2019). *The phenomenology of internal time-consciousness.* Indiana University Press.

Hvidt, E. A. (2017). The existential cancer journey: Travelling through the intersubjective structure of homeworld/alienworld. *Health, 21*(4), 375–391. https://doi.org/10.1177/1363459315617312

Javorská, A. (2016). Temporality and historicality of Dasein at Martin Heidegger. *Sincronía, 69,* 130–143.

Kaplan, T. (1982). Female consciousness and collective action: The case of Barcelona, 1910–1918. *Signs: Journal of Women in Culture and Society 7*(3), 545–566. https://doi.org/10.1086/493899

Keirby, A. C. S. (1997). Husserl's transcendental turn. *Journal of the British Society for Phenomenology,28*(2),204–215.https://doi.org/10.1080/00071773.1997.11007198

Kendler, K. S., & Parnas, J. (2008). *Philosophical issues in psychiatry. Explanation, phenomenology and nosology*. John Hopkins University Press.

Kockelmans, J. J. (1987). *Phenomenological psychology: The Dutch School*. Martinus Nijhoff Publishing.

Kockelmans, J. J., & Jager, B. (1967). *Edmund Husserl's phenomenological psychology: A historico-critical study*. Duquesne University Press.

Koloskov, D. (2022). Fundamental ontology, saturated phenomena and transcendental dilemma, *Journal of the British Society for Phenomenology* https://doi.org/10.1080/00071773.2022.2073247

Lagerkvist, A. (2017). Existential media: Toward a theorization of digital thrownness. *New Media & Society, 19*(1), 96–110. https://doi.org/10.1177/1461444816649921

Lambeth, M. (2021). Apperception (Apperzeption). In M. Wrathall (Ed.), *The Cambridge Heidegger lexicon* (pp. 50–52). Cambridge University Press. https://doi.org/10.1017/9780511843778.013

Lamont, M. (2004). A life of sad, but justified, choices: Interviewing across (too) many divides. In M. Bulmer & J. Solomos (Eds.), *Researching race and racism* (pp. 162–171). Routledge.

Langdridge, D. (2008). Phenomenology and critical social psychology: Directions and debates in theory and research. *Social and Personality Psychology Compass, 2*(3), 1126–1142. https://doi.org/10.1111/j.1751-9004.2008.00114.x

Larsen, H. G., & Adu, P. (2021). *The theoretical framework in phenomenological research: Development and application*. Routledge.

Larsen, H. G., & Wolowitz, L. (2015). A netnographic case study of Western expatriates' attitudes towards the Chinese in Shanghai. In M. J. Rozbicki (Ed.), *Perspectives on interculturality. The construction of meaning in relationship of difference* (pp. 179–204). Palgrave Macmillan.

Lohmar, D. (2014). Genetic phenomenology. In S. Luft & S. Overgaard (Eds.), *The Routledge companion to phenomenology* (pp. 266–275). Routledge.

Luft, S. (2004a). Husserl's Phenomenological reduction revisited: An attempt of a renewed account. *Anuario Filosófico, 37*(1), 65–104.

Luft, S. (2004b). Husserl's theory of the phenomenological reduction: Between life-world and cartesianims. *Research in Phenomenology, 32*(1), 198–234.

Luft, S. (2005). Husserl's concept of the transcendental person: Another look at the Husserl-Heidegger relationship. *International Journal of Philosophical Studies, 13*(2), 141–177. https://doi.org/10.1080/09672550500080371

Luft, S. (2011). Husserl's method of reduction. In S. Luft & S. Overgaard (Eds.), *The Routledge companion to phenomenology* (pp. 243–253). https://doi.org/10.4324/9780203816936.CH22

Maegher, T. (2021). The decolonial reduction and the transcendental-phenomenological reduction. *Philosophy and Global Affairs*, *1*(1), 72–96. https://doi.org/10.5840/pga2021282

Maldonado-Torres, N. (2022). Frantz Fanon and the decolonial turn in psychology: From modern/colonial methods to decolonial attitude. In L. Laubscher, D. Hook, & M. U. Desai (Eds.), *Fanon, phenomenology, and psychology* (pp. 89–99). Routledge.

Marder, M. (2011). The phenomenology of ontico-ontological difference. *Bulletin d'analyse Phenomenologique*, *8*(2), 1782–2041). http://popups.ulg.ac.be/bap.htm

Marder, M. 2014. *Phenomena-critique-logos: The project of critical phenomenology*. Rowman and Littlefield.

Marion, Jean-Luc (1998). *Reduction and givenness. Investigations of Husserl, Heidegger and phenomenology*. Northwestern University Press.

McBride, W. (2020). The look. In G. Weiss, A. V. Murphy, & G. Salamon (Eds.), *50 concepts for a critical phenomenology* (pp. 211–216). Northwestern University Press.

Meagher, T. (2021). Existential psychoanalysis and sociogeny. *Sartre Studies International*, 27(2), 48–59. https://doi.org/10.3167/ssi.2021.270206

Merleau-Ponty, M. (1967). *The structure of behavior*. Beacon Press.

Merleau-Ponty, M. (1978). *Phenomenology of perception*. Routledge & Kegan Paul.

Merleau-Ponty, M., Lefort, C., & Lingis, A. (1968). *The visible and the invisible followed by working notes*. Northwestern University Press.

Moran, D. (2000). *Introduction to phenomenology*. Routledge.

Moran, D. (2010). Husserl, Sartre and Merleau-Ponty on embodiment, touch and the double sensation. In K. J. Morris (Ed.), *Sartre on the body*. (pp. 41–66). Palgrave Macmillan.

Moustakas, C. E. (1994). *Phenomenological research methods*. Sage Publications.

Müller, M., Halová, D., Jedličková, L., & Cserge, T. (2022a). Existential disruptions of managers as a collapse of childhood patterns: An interpretative phenomenological investigation. *Integrative Psychological and Behavioral Science*, *56*, 779–800. https://doi.org/10.1007/s12124-021-09662-4

Müller, M., Jedličková, L., & Halová, D. (2022b). How do managers make sense of their crisis? Disrupted relationships and rediscovering co-existence. *Human Arenas: An Interdisciplinary Journal of Psychology, Culture, and Meaning*, 1–38. https://doi.org/10.1007/s42087-022-00272-z

Nørreklit, L. (2006). The double hermeneutics of life world: A perspective on the social, dialogue and interpretation. *Philosophy and Science Studies*, *5*, 1–13.

Oakley, A. (2016). Interviewing women again: Power, time and the gift. *Sociology*, *50*(1), 195–213. https://doi.org/10.1177/0038038515580253

Ofengenden, T. (2014). Memory formation and belief. *Dialogue in Philosophy, Mental and Neuro Sciences*, *7*(2), 34–44.

Okoroji, C., & Oka, E. (2021). Experiences of discrimination among black middle school adolescents: A qualitative study. *School Psychology*, *36*(6), 455–463. https://doi.org/10.1037/spq0000453.supp(Supplemental)

Oksala, J. (2006). A phenomenology of gender. *Continental Philosophy Review*, *39*(3), 229–244. https://doi.org/10.1007/s11007-006-9025-2.

Oksala, J. (2022). The method of critical phenomenology: Simone de Beauvoir as a phenomenologist. *European Journal of Philosophy*, 1–14. https://doi.org/10.1111/ejop.12782

Paley, J. (2014). Heidegger, lived experience and method. *Journal of Advanced Nursing*, *70*(7), 1520–1531. https://doi.org/10.1111/jan.12324

Paley, J. (2017). *Phenomenology as qualitative research*. Routledge.

Parker, D. M. (2015). *Sartre and no child left behind. An existential psychoanalytical anthropology of urban schooling*. Lexington Books.

Petitmengin, C. (2006). Describing one's subjective experience in the second person: An interview method for the science of consciousness. *Phenomenology and the Cognitive Sciences*, *5*, 229–269. http://dx.doi.org/10.1007/s11097-006-9022-2

Pollard, Christopher (2014). Is Merleau-Ponty's position in phenomenology of perception a new type of transcendental idealism? *Idealistic Studies*, *44*(1), 119–138. https://doi.org/10.5840/idstudies20152920

Proietti, M., Picksont, A., Graffitti, F., Barrow, P., Kundy, D., Branciard, C., Ringbauer, M., & Fedrizzi, A. (2019). Experimental test of local observer independence. *Science Advances*, *5*(9). https://doi.org/10.1126/sciadv.aaw9832

Rae, G. (2010). Re-thinking the human: Heidegger, fundamental ontology, and humanism. *Human Studies*, *33*, 23–39. https://doi.org/10.1007/s10746-010-9136-y

Ricoeur, P. (1979). The human experience of time and narrative. *Research in Phenomenology*, *9*(1), 17–34.

Ricoeur, P. (1994). *Oneself as another*. The University of Chicago Press.

Ricocur, P. (2019). *Hermeneutics and the human sciences*. Cambridge University Press.

Rodemeyer, L. M. (2020). The natural attitude. In G. Weiss, A. V. Murphy, & G. Salamon (Eds.), *50 concepts for a critical phenomenology* (pp. 3–9). Northwestern University Press.

Romano, C. (2012). Must phenomenology remain Cartesian? *Continental Philosophy Review*, *45*, 425–445.

Romdenh-Romluc, K. (2018). Science in Merleau-Ponty's phenomenology. In D. Zahavi (Ed.), *The Oxford handbook of the history of phenomenology* (pp. 340–359). Oxford University Press.

Rozbicki, M. J. (2015). Introduction: Intercultural studies: The methodological contours of an emerging discipline. In M. J. Rozbicki (Ed.), *Perspectives on interculturality. The construction of meaning in relationship of difference* (pp. 1–23). Palgrave Macmillan.

Salamon, G. (2018a). What's critical about critical phenomenology? *Puncta Journal of Critical Phenomenology*, *1*(1), 8–17. https://doi.org/10.31608/PJCP.v1i1.2

Salamon, G. (2018b). *The life and death of Latisha King: A critical phenomenology of transphobia.* NYU Press. https://doi.org/10.2307/j.ctvfb6z5z

Sartre, J. P. (1991). *The psychology of imagination.* Citadel Press.

Sartre, J. P. (1992). *Being and nothingness.* Washington Square Press.

Sartre, J. P. (2001). *The transcendence of the ego. An existentialist theory of the ego.* Hill and Wang.

Sartre, J. P. (2007). *Existentialism is a humanism.* Yale University Press.

Scheler, M. (1954). *The nature of sympathy.* Yale University Press.

Scheler, M. (1973). *Formalism in ethics and non-formal ethics of values.* Northwestern University Press.

Scheler, M. (2009). *The human place in the cosmos.* Northwestern University Press.

Schrödinger, E. (2019). *What is life?* Cambridge University Press.

Schutz, A. (1972). *The phenomenology of the social world.* Northwestern University Press.

Scott-Baumann, A. (2012). *Ricoeur and the hermeneutics of suspicion.* Continuum.

Sheehan, T. (2007). *Huserl-Heidegger Correspondance, 1914–1934. Becoming Heidegger: On the trail of his early occasional writings.* https://www.academia.edu/39557451/HUSSERL-HEIDEGGER_CORRESPONDENCE_1914-1934

Simonsen, K. & Koefod, L. (2020). *Geographies of embodiment.* Sage.

Smith, J. A., Flowers, P., & Larkin, M. (2009). *Interpretative phenomenological analysis: Theory, method and research.* Sage Publications.

Sousa, D. (2014). Phenomenological psychology: Husserl's static and genetic methods. *Journal of Phenomenological Psychology, 45*(1), 27–60. https://doi.org/10.1163/15691624-12341267

Sousa, D. (2017). *Existential psychotherapy: A genetic-phenomenological approach.* Palgrave Macmillan.

Spiegelberg, H. (1971). *The phenomenological movement. A historical introduction* (2nd ed.). Springer Science + Business Media, BV.

Steinbock, A. J. (1995). *Home and beyond: Generative phenomenology after Husserl.* Northwestern University Press.

Steinbock, A. J. (1998). Husserl's static and genetic phenomenology: Translator's introduction to two essays. Essay 1: Static and genetic phenomenological method. Essay 2: The phenomenology of monadic individuality and the phenomenology of the general possibilities and compossibilities of lived-experiences: Static and genetic phenomenology. *Continental Philosophy Review, 31,* 127–152. https://doi.org/10.1023/A:1010089123758

Steup, M. (2008). Epistemology in the twentieth century. In D. Moran (Ed.), *The Routledge companion to twentieth century philosophy* (pp. 469–521). Routledge. https://doi.org/10.4324/9780203879368

Stilwell, P., & Harman, K. (2019). An enactive approach to pain: Beyond the biopsychosocial model. *Phenomenology and the Cognitive Sciences, 18,* 637–665. https://doi.org/10.1007/s11097-019-09624-7

Thompson, E., & Zahavi, D. (2007). Philosophical issues: Phenomenology. In *The Cambridge Handbook of Consciousness* (pp. 67–88). Cambridge University Press. https://doi.org/10.1017/CBO9780511816789.005

Thun, R. (2010). Ricoeur on self-constitution by alterity-experience. Hermeneutical dimensions of the fractured cogito. In E. B. Pires, B. Nonnenmacher, & S. Büttner-Von Stülpnagel (Eds.), *Relations of the self* (pp. 333–348). Imprensa da Universidade de Coimbra.

Thwaites, R. (2017). (Re)examining the feminist interview: Rapport, gender "matching," and emotional labour. *Frontiers in Sociology, 2*(18) https://doi.org/10.3389/fsoc.2017.00018

Tymieniecka, A-T. (2006). Unveiling the logos of scientific interrogation. In A-T. Tymieniecka (Ed.), *Analecta Husserliana: Logos of phenomenology and phenomenology of the logos. Book four: The logos of scientific interrogation* (pp. xi–xvi). Springer.

Vagle, M. D. (2018). *Crafting phenomenological research* (2nd ed.). Routledge.

Van Manen, M. (2007). Phenomenology of practice. *Phenomenology & Practice, 1*(1), 11–30.

Van Manen, M. (2016). *Phenomenology of practice: Meaning-giving methods in phenomenological research and writing.* Taylor & Francis.

Van Manen, M. (2017). Phenomenology in its original sense. *Qualitative Health Research, 27*(6), 810–825. https://doi.org/10.1177/1049732317699381

Vermersch, P. (2017). *The explication interview* (English translation of L'entretien D'explicitation. ESF Éditeur).

Vogt, K. M. (2012). *Belief and truth: A skeptic reading of Plato.* Oxford University Press.

Wang, X. (2020). The digital Dasein of Chinese rural migrants. *Sociologia & Antropologia, 10*(3), 807–830. https://doi.org/10.1590/2238-38752020v1032

Warren, N. D. (2014). Time. In S. Luft & S. Overgaard (Eds.), *The Routledge companion to phenomenology* (pp. 190–201). Routledge.

Webber, J. (2018). *Rethinking existentialism.* OUP Oxford.

Weiss, G., Murphy, A. V., & Salamon, G. (2020). Introduction: Transformative descriptions. In G. Weiss, A. V. Murphy, & G. Salamon (Eds.), *50 concepts for a critical phenomenology* (pp. xii–xiv). Northwestern University Press.

Welang, N. (2018). Triple consciousness: The reimagination of Black female identities in contemporary American culture. *Open Cultural Studies, 2*(1), 296–306. https://doi.org/10.1515/culture-2018-0027

Welsh, T. (2022). *Feminist existentialism, biopolitics, and critical phenomenology in a time of bad health.* Routledge.

Welton, D. (2003). The systematicity of Husserl's transcendental philosophy. From static to genetic method. In D. Welton (Ed.), *The new Husserl. A critical reader* (pp. 255–288). Indiana University Press.

Wertz, F. J. (1985). Method and findings in a phenomenological psychological study of a complex life-event: Being criminally victimized. In A. Giorgi (Ed.), *Phenomenology and psychological research* (pp. 155–216). Duquesne University Press.

Wertz, F. J., & Greenhut, J. M. (1985). A psychology of buying: Demonstration of a phenomenological approach in consumer research. *Advances in Consumer Research, 12*(1), 566–570.

Wilde L. (2022). Trauma: Phenomenological causality and implication. *Phenomenology & The Cognitive Sciences.* *21*(3), 689–705. https://doi. org/10.1007/s11097-020-09725-8

Wilshire, B. (1969). Protophenomenology in the psychology of William James. *Transactions of the Charles S. Peirce Society*, *5*(1), 25–43.

Young, A. A. (2004). Experiences in ethnographic interviewing about race: The inside and outside of it. In M. Blumer & J. Solomos (Eds.), *Researching race and racism* (pp. 187–202). Routledge.

Zahavi, D. (2007). Subjectivity and the first person perspective. *Southern Journal of Philosophy*, *45*, 66–84. https://doi.org/10.1111/j.2041-6962.2007. tb00113.x

Zahavi, D. (2008a). Phenomenology. In D. Moran (Ed.), *The Routledge companion to twentieth century philosophy* (pp. 661–692).

Zahavi, D. (2018b). Getting it quite wrong: Van Manen and Smith on phenomenology. *Qualitative Health Research*, *29*(6), 900–907. https://doi. org/10.1177/1049732318817547

Zahavi, D. (2018c). Introduction. In D. Zahavi (Ed.), *The Oxford handbook of the history of phenomenology* (pp. 1–2) Oxford University Press.

Zahavi, D. (2019). Applied phenomenology: Why it is safe to ignore the epoché. *Continental Philosophy Review*, 1–15. https://doi.org/10.1007/ s11007-019-09463-y

Index

Pages in *italics* refer figures.

For Product Safety Concerns and Information please contact our EU
representative GPSR@taylorandfrancis.com
Taylor & Francis Verlag GmbH, Kaufingerstraße 24, 80331 München, Germany

www.ingramcontent.com/pod-product-compliance
Lightning Source LLC
Chambersburg PA
CBHW050532270326
41926CB00015B/3188